CW01501317

"A Gre
Alan Waugh's *Alchemical Ayahuasc*
Ayahuasca. It is, first and foremost
love distilled through many years (
is a friendly book. It is an honest book. It is a practical book. It is a
book of gentle, persuasive power. It is a book of revelations. And it is a
kindly book that will take your hand with confidence and help you find
your own path out of pain and into healing.

~ GRAHAM HANCOCK

Best Selling Author of *Fingerprints of the Gods*, *Visionary*,
America Before, Creator and Presenter of No.1 Netflix Series—
Ancient Apocalypse

"In *Alchemical Ayahuasca* Alan Waugh takes the reader on a long and
highly detailed account of his personal journey from depression to
a happier and fulfilled life. Leaving seemingly no stone along his
personal path unturned, Alan describes the guidance of an inner voice
dubbed Amantane, which directs him to make radical changes in
virtually all of his life circumstances. He encounters yogis of India and
shamans of South America who assist him in his self-discovery and
integration. This is a tale of personal recovery, set amidst a myriad of
atypical and challenging circumstances."

~ CHRIS KILHAM

Educator, Researcher of plant-based medicines
and Author of *The Ayahuasca Test Pilots Handbook*,
Tales from The Medicine Trail, *The Five Tibetans*

"Alan Waugh is a dedicated healer of many modalities and brings a
deep presence to all of his offerings. He is a master at holding safe and
sacred space for the deepest healing and awakening to take place. His
reverence, devotion, and refined attention are truly remarkable! This
book, *Alchemical Ayahuasca*, will bring a great blessing to the World,
demystifying the sacred Ayahuasca Journey and establishing it as an
important medicine for today's challenges of depression and anxiety."

~ ASHANNA SOLARIS

Co-Founder of CLARITY BREATHWORK

ALCHEMICAL
AYAHUASCA

ISBN 978-1-962213-00-4

Edited and designed by Dianna Jerrybandhan
Interior typesetting by Jess LaGreca, Mayfly Design
Cover design by Rica Graphics

Published by Chakana Publishing

Disclaimer: The author does not hold
responsibility for your health choices.

Printed in the United States of America
First printing edition September 2023

For more information, contact the author at
www.alchemicalayahuasca.com

Proudly written without the use of (AI) Artificial Intelligence.

ALCHEMICAL AYAHUASCA

Take the Journey
from Depression to The Sweet Spot

ALAN FRANCIS WAUGH

CONTENTS

FOREWORD

With the unpretentious wisdom of a seasoned healer and the spellbinding eloquence of a skillful storyteller, Alan Waugh, my trusted friend and cherished shamanic soul ally in the Great Work, has accomplished something extraordinary in writing *Alchemical Ayahuasca: Take the Journey from Depression to the Sweet Spot*.

A compelling blend of personal memoir and hero's quest, reading *Alchemical Ayahuasca* takes us on a magical mystery tour of a life reshaped by sacred encounters with non-ordinary dimensions of evolutionary consciousness.

Moreover, *Alchemical Ayahuasca* unveils the captivating world of Ayahuasca-based plant medicine shamanism, where the author's personal experiences provide a uniquely authentic and transparent glimpse into the healing potential of this time-honored Amazonian plant sacrament practice.

When we look at Ayahuasca from Waugh's personal experiences and challenges, we can see how it deeply influences the path to self-acceptance and spiritual growth. The author's wisdom gained from participating in and facilitating hundreds of ceremonies, is an invaluable guide for newcomers and consummate Ayahuasca psychonauts.

In visionary alignment with the tribal prophecies spoken around council fires by our original peoples since time immemorial, this excellent book is a poignant reminder that it is our evolutionary purpose to flower in consciousness, by looking deeply into our inner worlds. The author takes a close-up look at the negative sides of human behavior and encourages readers to reflect on their own limitations. He also explains the spiritual reasons behind unhealthy behaviors and thought patterns.

Alan Waugh's metaphor of learning to sing at a higher pitch by first learning to sing at a lower pitch, beautifully encapsulates our spiritual journey in human form. From the depths of despair and crippling depression to the heights of pure happiness and liberating freedom, this uniquely insightful book is a triumphant testament to the power of human resilience and the wisdom gained through adversity.

Alchemical Ayahuasca conveys a universal truth: happiness, peace, love, abundance, and health already exist within us. They coexist with fear, anger, lack, disease, and suffering. The dominant force in our lives depends on our choices. Reading it transports us to a meditative space that ignites the imagination. It's a fortuitous odyssey that promises to enrich lives, expand consciousness, and inspire a newfound perspective characterized by kindness, compassion, and soul-awakened empowerment—a simple, yet powerful path to positive transformational magic!

In essence, this remarkable book is intended to serve both those new to shamanic studies and experienced practitioners, by centering on ways to establish supportive visionary partnerships of healing grace, with seen and unseen multidimensional powers and forces that are complementary—some would say necessary—to our current human existence and evolution. It offers time-proven practices artfully designed to awaken various states of shamanic consciousness that nurture our soul's maturation into Shining Ones—beings of light and love, walking with beauty on our cherished Earth.

I predict *Alchemical Ayahuasca: Take the Journey from Depression to the Sweet Spot* shall rapidly emerge as a vital resource and significant guide among all dedicated to safeguarding the sanctity and healthful flourishing of life on Earth—*Hinayá!*

Oscar Miro-Quesada is a respected kamasqa curandero and altomisayoq adept from Peru, a Fellow in Ethnopsychology with the Organization of American States, Invited Observer to the United Nations Forum on Indigenous Issues, originator of Pachakuti Mesa Tradition cross-cultural shamanism, Founder of The Heart of the Healer Shamanic Mystery School www.theheartofthehealer.org, author of *Shamanism: Personal Quests of Communion with Nature and Creation; Healing Light* (Sounds True), and *Lessons in Courage: Peruvian Shamanic Wisdom for Everyday Life.*

ACKNOWLEDGEMENTS

I live a beautiful life.

It has not always been that way.

The start of my life shift from depression to happiness began at age 28, when in the midst of an existential crisis, I received teachings from a benevolent Voice for the first time. I did not know if this was the Voice from my innate wisdom, my higher self, or from an autonomous being. That was not important. What was vitally important was that I listened to the Voice and took action. Those actions have led me to where I am today—living a fulfilled life, while helping others live in their highest potential. That Voice has been an ally of mine ever since.

Since the mid 1990's I have studied with many luminaries in the healing arts to whom I owe a great debt of gratitude: to Michael Harner and Hank Wesselman for introducing me to core shamanic practices. Words aren't enough to thank Don Oscar Miro Quesada, Kamasqa Curandero from Peru, who has always supported me with his inspirational ceremonial teachings, mentoring and Artes (medicine pieces) from his direct lineage. Thanks to all the Shipibo Maestros and Maestras of the Peruvian Jungle who have guided me through many years of Ayahuasca ceremonies.

Much gratitude to my now deceased friend Cielo Tierra in Pucallpa, Peru, for being such a rock of care, nurturing and inspiration through many years of friendship. I dedicate this book to you.

Deep gratitude to my dear friend Nicole Doherty for being my partner in ceremony for seven years. Heartfelt gratitude to my spiritual brother Biré, Pajé Shaman of the Huni Kuin Tribe in Brazil, whose laughter and lightness of spirit fill my soul.

Immense gratitude to Graham, Santha and Sean Hancock, for your many referrals and continued support over the years. Thank you to Goddesses Ashanna Solaris and Dana de Long for guiding me so lovingly through Clarity Breathwork training and showing me how to hold space with such deep love.

A special thank you to Barbara Snow for your editorial assistance. Thank you to my friend Roy Remer for your excellent suggestions.

Profound gratitude to Ayahuasca Zen Master, don Ignacio Diuri for teaching me that *life doesn't have to be that hard,* which has helped me re-frame my whole life ethos.

A deep bow of love to all the hundreds of deceased teachers who allowed me to become a better me through sitting at your bedside for over twenty years of hospice volunteering. I am humbled by the power of that work and by your grace. Thank you to the Zen Hospice Project for your trainings and support.

Thank you to the thousands of clients and friends who trusted me to hold your hands on the path to wellness.

Infinite gratitude to Mount Shasta, the powerful sacred mountain in Northern California where I have lived and worked at my retreat center Sacred Valley Spiritual Retreat, for the last seven years and to the Sacred Valley in Ecuador where I now live and plan to spend the rest of my days.

Thank you to my dear Mother Mary Lamb Waugh for giving birth to me and continuing to be a source of inspiration by how you live your life—with such enthusiasm and positivity— I Love You.

My deepest gratitude to my Beloved, Dianna Jerrybandhan Waugh for holding my hand on this path. This book would not have been written if it weren't for your love, support and encouragement. Apu Shasta brought us together to do great work. I love you and the journey we are on together, with all my heart.

Thank you to the plant spirits of Ayahuasca and Huachuma for giving me my most powerful healing tools and teaching me so much more!

Lastly, to honor myself and my journey I give thanks to me—Alan, for being willing to persevere and trust myself with the choices I made and my commitment to them. I kept true to myself, my path of service and service to the collective. I love you with every cell of my being.

PREFACE

The great work!

I have practiced with many *Maestros* (master healers) primarily in Peru. When I asked them how I could do something, how do I endure the challenges in life, how do I gain mastery in a particular practice, or learn all the prayers, the medicine songs, etc., they universally answered me in the same way—
"Necesitas dominar, Alan!"—"You have to dominate, Alan!"

A better translation of that phrase to a Westerner, might be, *you have to elevate yourself.* Elevate yourself above the doubts you have around being able to learn, or the challenges you feel there are in your studies. Raise the bar of your commitment and push forward with the perseverance that is required in any area of achieving a high level of mastery. The questions I posed to them did not come from a place of confidence, or inner strength. They were questions that already held the energy of doubt and self-sabotage.

Sometimes they didn't say anything, they just raised an eyebrow with a quizzical look, as though they didn't understand the question—it seemed alien to them.

They seemed to say, *"if you want to do something, then do it"*. They are jungle people of few words around their own healing prowess. Their sense of rationale was so different to mine and sometimes I felt as though they were hiding their wisdom from me or being evasive. The truth is, they learn by observation and if something needs doing, they simply do it, otherwise it doesn't get done.

The short answer they universally gave me, *necesitas dominar*, held in it everything I needed and more, to let me know they had no time for timewasters. They answered with firm kindness. Their responses contained strength and clarity and they didn't need to express more for me to understand. It is unnecessary to say anything more to someone who is ready to follow a challenging path, a path which they simply see as training, an apprenticeship. The maestros wanted to see nothing less than my full commitment to be a carrier of their medicine ways.

In the pages that follow, you will receive a distillation of lessons learnt on my spiritual path, guided by my own extraordinary experiences. I have simplified a lot of the lessons here to help your healing journey be an easier one than mine.

Alchemical Ayahuasca contains stories from my extensive experience with the Master Plant Teacher known as Ayahuasca, in the tradition that I primarily learnt in—the Shipibo tradition. Ayahuasca is known by many names (Yajé, Daime, Natem, Caapi, Nixie Pae, etc.), depending on the culture and language where it is used.

Ayahuasca helped me to access the deepest parts of my Self and still guides me today in changing the parts that still need a bit of work.

She continues to show me that the most effective way to live fully is the path of least resistance. Any other way causes too many challenges, too much stress. I learnt that I didn't have to climb the emotional mountain, or travel to distant lands to surmount my challenges; I could simply stay where I was. What was required, was for me to be fully present where I was, willing to commit and invest in myself to make changes that support the easiest path to wellness and happiness.

The humble path that I am following is not part of my cultural lineage. Over the years I have studied with maestros and maestras, sometimes living in their homes and they have shared their time, their traditions and their medicine with me willingly. I have paid them generously in *sacred reciprocity*. They have always treated me, and I have always treated them and their traditions, with great respect. We mutually share a deep interest in the healing of *Pachamama* (Earth) and all her relations.

This is a path you too can follow to achieve similar outcomes and decide whether Ayahuasca is to be part of that path. This book will I hope, help to illustrate some of the benefits and some of the pitfalls.

I incorporate in this book an overview of some human conditions and what I consider the challenging aspects or attributes of it. Also included are simple exercises and practices to help *dominar* or elevate you beyond them. By the end of this book, you will hopefully have learnt techniques that will transform your life.

In my practice, I have always felt that you have to work on extracting the Dark to allow room for the Light, not just simply call in the light, as there would not be any room for it. The dark has to be exposed and expelled, through initially doing *shadow work*.

I have also learnt that the light does not always transform the dark. Positivity does not always transform negativity. Suffering is not necessarily transformed by compassion. They all co-exist. The light co-exists with the dark. Your fear and your love occupy the same vessel simultaneously. This book will teach you how the light will transcend the darkness—with your help. You will be much happier for it.

Alchemical Ayahuasca contains lessons that Ayahuasca has taught me about myself and how I can help others heal with or without drinking Ayahuasca. Drinking Aya can be a very challenging process; you will read some of the stories here. I will also show you an easier way.

The post-Ayahuasca experience, better known as *integration*, is often the biggest part of one's transformational journey. This book was written for novices and also for those of you who have already embarked on this work, to help you integrate your plant medicine experiences or other healing processes. Exercises and wisdoms shared in Part III are helpful with integration.

What is required from you is your commitment
to the easiest path of transformation,
and you too will live a beautiful life.

INTRODUCTION

Life is really simple,
But we insist on making it complicated.
~ CONFUCIUS

THIS BOOK HAS BEEN WRITTEN IN 3 PARTS

Part I: The Journey Begins is part-memoir and part-hero's journey as I learned ways of living differently, leading me to what has turned out to be an exceptional life.

It explains how I moved from a place of deep depression to a place of expanding into happiness. I walked the path of the Wounded Healer, so I can speak directly from my experiences and particularly my challenges to illustrate how they brought me deep wisdom. This was the training ground to my fulfillment.

Part II: The Alchemy of Ayahuasca is about my introduction to the incredible world of Ayahuasca Shamanism and the experiences that drew me into this fascinating ancient way of healing. I recount some of my earlier experiences, which though unique to me, may give the un-initiated a sense of how Ayahuasca helps you to face your fears and in so doing, learn to Love yourself more. The *bitch slaps* that brought me to my knees during my medicine journeys were my greatest teachers of humility and wisdom.

I draw on my experience of sitting in several hundred ceremonies, both with groups and on my own—to share my theories on how Ayahuasca heals. I suggest how to learn from your experiences and precautionary measures when considering embarking on this journey. This part is helpful for Ayahuasca virgins as well as, experienced drinkers.

Part III: The Easy Path is about my personal philosophy and some of techniques I have learnt for healing. It also contains processes that were taught to me by Ayahuasca over nearly two decades, that I use to change people's lives in my work as a healer, teacher and plant medicine ceremonialist.

I share a few client stories in this section to illustrate the variety of ways in which these processes can help you. I have changed all of the names except for the story about my friend Lise.

I share a number of simple yet powerful exercises to help you transform your life and take you to the sweet spot of healing! The healing process is subtle: it is beautiful: it is deep. Once you enter the healing mode, it continues on its own.

In this part we journey into a more expansive, meditative place that will engage your imagination. It is a fun journey and one I hope will enrich your life, expand your awareness and help you see your life in a whole new way—a way of softness, of kindness and of self-empowerment. It is a way of Magic!

The Appendix gives a brief description of the beliefs and working systems of people who operate within the Shamanic Paradigm. *Shaman* is an often mis-used term and I include this part to clarify its meaning.

PART I

My Journey Begins

THE VOICE—*that changed my life!*

Life shrinks or expands
In proportion to one's courage.
~ ANAÏS NIN

I was Suicidal.

I was 28 years old, living in Croydon, a suburb of South London. I had been working in the building industry for the last six years and was the owner of a small construction company that primarily focused on renovating Victorian houses in the area; there are a lot of them in London and therefore I was very busy.

As a workaholic, I was working a lot and doing my best to manage a few troublesome employees. Financially I was doing the best I had done up to that point in my life but I was feeling desperate. I mistakenly thought that money would be the source of happiness, but having money in the bank made no difference to my challenging mental states.

Day after day, I was plummeting into the depths of hopelessness, with no way out from my negative mind space. Being only 28, I didn't have the life experience, wisdom, or awareness for figuring out how to be happy. I perceived my world and my future as hopeless. I was not in a relationship; I did not love myself, let alone even like myself. I was masterful in self-criticism and self-shaming and I was moving on the treadmill of life believing that happiness would never be a reality for me, only different degrees of unhappiness.

I recognize today, with hindsight, that I had been depressed since ages 10 or 11 and possibly even earlier. I lived in a family where we weren't encouraged to talk about our feelings. Despite having four sisters, I always felt alone, and outside of work, I kept myself fairly isolated. My best friends were a bottle of wine, self-rolled hashish cigarettes, speed pills and a cute little grey cockatiel bird named Beaker. I had suicidal ideation from a young age and can remember thinking I would be dead by sixteen.

I was ready to leave this life—not realizing that I was about to leave *this life*, but not in the way I expected.

A VOICE IN MY HEAD

One typically dreary day in London, I found myself sitting on the floor in my apartment where I lived alone, feeling desperately unhappy and with no hope of a brighter future. This for me was just the course of my life: a predetermined reality, deigned by God. With waves of depression rolling over and through me, I knew this was the day I would end my life.

From out of nowhere a Voice spoke to me! It sounded like the Voice was outside of me, but I couldn't be sure. It was a male Voice, strong and clear. He said,

"Do you want to live, or do you want to die?"

I was taken aback but felt it was a serious question that I needed to respond to. In my despair, there was only one answer to give: *I want to die!*

Even though this was a unique experience in my life and far out of my normal frame of reference, I took it in stride because it felt completely natural.

Again, He asked, **"Do you want to Live, or do you want to Die?"**

This time, I knew He meant business so I searched deeper inside myself, into the source of my pain—deeper than I had ever given myself permission to go before. Up to that point I had grown accustomed to wallowing in self-pity and had become resigned to a life of hopelessness. In that moment, I began moving beyond mental reasoning—to a state of being. I began *soul searching*. I was connecting with a place deep in my core that I had not accessed before. Previously, I was always stuck in my head, trapped in patterns of despair. Not only was the Voice talking to me but, the source of that Voice was guiding me in how to look inside myself, literally to the heart of the matter: to the heart of myself.

I took this question: *Do you want to Live or do you want to Die*, into a new realm of experience—a feeling experience, beyond my egoic patterning and conditioning. I quickly began to experience a gentler, more spacious and open relationship to myself, which was markedly different from my old rigid and fixed views. I was being gently guided to really look beyond the me that I knew.

In the gentleness and expansiveness of that moment, I connected to Love.

Instantly, I knew I had a choice to make: either keep believing that unhappiness was my normal operating system (my old conditioning), or make a different, unfamiliar choice, where I had full sovereignty over my life outcome.

I responded: *I want to Live! I want to Live! But how do I Live, I am so unhappy? How can I continue to endure such pain?*

"I'm going to tell you." The kind Voice responded.

"You have to change the patterns of your life. Actions have consequences and if you continue to live your life the way you have been living, then nothing will change."

Upon hearing that, I shrunk back into my fears, worrying that I would not be able to move away from the negative beliefs that felt comfortable and familiar. I quickly reviewed my life and asked: *But what about the last 15 years of my life? Am I just going to give that up? If I just move out of depression, then all of those years will have been for nothing? All of those years will be wasted and lost?*

The Voice responded, **"Who cares—just You?"**

It was simple, powerful and life changing.

I realized in that moment that I had been attached to beliefs I was using to keep myself small. I was afraid of life. I was using my depression as a crutch to support myself on my journey into smallness—to hide myself away and not be seen. I realized I was being given a choice—a choice to break out of my cocoon of misery that allowed me to feel safe.

It's true, only I cared. Why live the rest of my life in misery, just because I didn't want to let go of the past suffering of fifteen or sixteen years, during which time I believed that I wasn't lovable? In that moment I realized that I had become addicted to my depression and I remained addicted to give myself a distorted purpose for my life.

I laughed at the ridiculousness of it all.

That laugh was the first big energetic release of density and overwhelm that I let myself feel in over fifteen years. The energy shift of that release has guided me on my path of happiness ever since.

THE POWER OF LAUGHTER

For as long as I could remember up to that point, I had been the Joker, the Comic. When out with friends, I was always the one with the quickest wit. I wanted people to laugh around me: to validate me as the funny one, the Wise Cracker. I was in competition with my drinking buddies to be the funniest joker. Otherwise, I was introverted, quiet and painfully shy. Making self-disparaging or sarcastic remarks and being the source of humor was my way of relating to the world without giving away my secret—

I am depressed and I feel terrible about myself.

I was a sad clown who wore a mask and cloak of happiness. My jollity was a form of self-medication and like so many comics—I was a depressed funny man.

That density releasing laugh, was liberating. It felt good to be real and honest at last. That laugh was a panacea to my inner conflict, my inner delusion and it quickly became a catalyst for a truer version of myself.

BEING TRUE TO MYSELF

When I responded, *I want to Live!* I knew I was going to have to live in a radically new way. I was going to have to step out of my comfort zone of depression and live life more fully beyond the limited parameters I had set for myself. It felt scary, but it also felt like my deep truth.

It was a transformative moment in my life—within the blink of an eye—to realize I had *a choice.* I had a choice beyond anything I had imagined up to that point. My choice, I decided, was to live.

But how do I do that? How do I change the actions of my life, so that I am no longer depressed and only want to die? I asked.

"I'm going to tell you" the Voice responded. "You are going to leave England. You are going to leave the heavy influence that this country and culture has had on you. You are going on a journey to find yourself, a spiritual adventure that will expand your current awareness of reality. You will step out into the world and explore the vastness of belief systems and cultures that exist outside your bubble of conditioning. It will be uncomfortable, it won't be easy, but the challenges of the journey and the explorations both physical and metaphysical are what you need to walk into a new way of living, a new way of relating to yourself. You will feel hopeful: you will learn how to experience deep happiness!"

He continued . . . .

"You are going to travel the world for 18 months. You will explore new cultures and meet many people on their own journeys. You are going to be out there on your own in the big, wide world and you will learn what it is to be truly Free!"

YES! I responded.

In that moment, I knew I was being given a directive—that would alter my life significantly. A hero's journey, before I even knew what that meant and I immediately affirmed that I was willing to do what it took.

I knew instinctively I was going to start my journey in India.

GETTING CLEAR WITH MYSELF

What I tapped into, in that soul-searching process offered to me by my Spirit Guide, (he could be described as an Angel), is what I later saw as me setting clear boundaries with and for myself. I have since learnt that I can only set clear boundaries when I tap into an inherent strength that is beyond the place of rational thought.

I realize that when I try to think my way to a solution, I often connect with self-doubt and stir up beliefs that created the problem in the first place.

I had been raised in a traditional Catholic family and taught by Nuns and Monks through my whole schooling—Kindergarten to High School. Through the influence of their teachings, I believed that I had sinned against God. After all, why was I so miserable? I must have sinned against God. Why was I unlovable? Because God didn't love me! I also believed that I was not allowed to question any act of God.

Even though I had moved away from Christianity at age 16, I was still holding on to the conditioning I received from a very early age. To make my own life choices, to recognize that my life path was fully determined by the actions that I took, was an alien concept to me. I later learnt that this concept was a central Buddhist teaching, sometimes described as the Law of Karma.

I realized in that moment of clarity, that I had full responsibility for my own happiness. This was a significant insight.

Three months after that initial interaction with my Spirit Guide, I gave the construction company to my business partner Brian and set off from Victoria Station, London, on an eighteen-month journey into the unknown.

INTO THE UNKNOWN—*India*

Leap and your wings will unfurl.

~ A.F.W.

Several old friends came to Victoria Train Station to bid me farewell over a pint of beer—or two! None of my friends had ever done anything like this. I felt nervous and I didn't have a clue about what I was getting into; all I had was a one-way ticket to Delhi. Part of me wanted to stay here and drown my sorrows in a few more pints. My only experience of travel outside of England had been short vacations to Ireland to visit my mother's family and a month in France on a language and culture exchange during high school.

Despite the fears and concerns of my friends and family, who thought I was nuts to leave a business that was *successful* and a life that was *comparatively comfortable*, I was single focused on my journey ahead. I desperately wanted to release my self-anger, negative self-talk and self-criticism, but more strongly, I wanted to find the source of happiness and fulfillment.

I somehow knew that the courage it would take for me to set foot away from my familiar life into the unknown, would be a pivotal part of my healing journey. Just to go, was a mas-

10

sive leap of growth towards a new and better version of myself. What I was actually leaping into though—the void—scared the shit out of me.

I didn't have a road map. I didn't buy a guidebook. I just stepped into the world ready to explore and experience whatever this journey held in store for me, knowing that Delhi, India was my starting point.

I did though, have a spiritual ally with whom I was developing a trusting relationship. I now know his name is *Amantane* (a-mun-tan-ay) and he has been a beloved counsel ever since.

INSTANT VEGETARIAN

Landing at Delhi airport in February of 1986 was marked by a large and raggedy troupe of baboons running across the runway as the plane wheels slowed to a halt. When the cabin door opened, I was hit in the face by a dense wall of heat.

Now what was I going to do? I didn't even have a hotel room booked. I felt nervous but also quite liberated. I hooked up with a fellow traveler from the plane and we had a taxi driver take us into an area with cheap hotels.

A client of mine had loaned me a travel memoir set in India, *The Great Railway Bazaar* by Paul Theroux, which gave me a little insight into the colorful street scenes of India. So, in a small way I had a sense of what I would witness here—a kaleidoscope of color and overstimulation of the senses.

On this first morning after having breakfast at my hotel, I wandered the streets around New Delhi Railway Station. As I walked around and took in the sights and sounds, nothing in Theroux's book could have prepared me for the overwhelming mixture of noises, incredible aromas, and vibrant array of colors, of India. I carefully stepped around the cows lying on the streets, with heaps of dung littering the sidewalks, whilst doing my best to avoid the profusion of tuk-tuk motor bike taxis that were everywhere. They moved like a shoal of fish in an intuitive choreographed flow, miraculously never hitting each other. It was incredible.

I meandered along the bustling streets and noticed down the road ahead of me a large white Marquee, in front of which hung a huge amorphous black cloud; it was strangely moving and shifting in the air outside the tent.

As I drew closer, I realized that it was a swarm of thousands of black flies. This was a butcher's market! On entering the tent, I observed why the flies were so abundant; there were huge slabs of meat on the marble countertops, sweltering in the immense heat. There was no refrigeration. The flies formed a thick layer and covered the meat. I felt sick to my stomach.

Next, my eyes shifted to the floor where I looked aghast at the chickens cooped up in small pens and large live fish, squeezed into small plastic buckets—with more flies buzzing around everything.

When a customer chose a chicken, it got pulled from the pen and had its head cut off with a hatchet. Its body was then thrown into an oil drum, where the chicken went through its death throws—its blood spurting up and all over the walls. In that moment, Amantane spoke to me and very clearly said,

"If you eat meat in this country, you will die!"

This was obviously meant to impress upon me the danger of eating meat in such unsanitary and inhumane conditions.

Without hesitation—I responded: YES!

I became an instant vegetarian. Back in England I was an ardent meat eater—I had never considered becoming a vegetarian. I often ate meat in some form, three times a day, almost at every meal. This was no small decision. Fortunately, I was in the best country in the world to give up eating meat, where over 50% of the huge population ate vegetarian or vegan diets.

This was a choice I made from that light within me that represented a growing confidence that was guiding me more and more.

At the time of writing, I have not eaten meat for thirty-seven years.

THE MAHA KUMBH MELA

I came on my journey to have the biggest experiences that I could and my arrival in India could not have been timed any better for that to happen—in spades.

As *luck* would have it, I landed in India at a time which coincided with the largest Hindu festival, which is also the largest spiritual festival in the world—the Maha Kumbh Mela. This renowned festival takes place *every twelve years*, and it was happening not far from Delhi! The Kumbh Mela is a Hindu festival where holy men and women, known as Saddhus, bathe in the Sacred River Ganges at the ceremony site. This ancient practice is done to honor the Hindu Deity Lord Shiva and is believed to help a person achieve *moksha* or salvation. Hindus believe that one bath in the Ganges River during the full moon at the Kumbh Mela, is equivalent to the blessing of ten thousand holy baths at other times.

I headed up to the giant festival and to my delight, discovered I didn't have to travel all over India to experience Hindu spirituality—it had come to me! Many of the travelers I met there had come to India specifically to attend this amazing event, yet I had never heard of it until I arrived.

The town of Haridwar on the Ganges River at most other times is a sleepy place of pilgrimage for devotees of Lord Shiva.

When the Kumbh Mela comes to town, it swells by tens of millions of devotees from all over the subcontinent, as well as, other parts of the world. Haridwar transforms into a bourgeoning sea of religious devotion.

Hundreds of thousands of Saddhus, covered with white ash, packed tented encampments on the banks of the Ganges, smoking pipes known as chillums, filled with hashish. These holy men are often completely naked, with dreadlocks piled on top their heads, which look like hairy termites' nests.

There were many festivities going on, including lavish processions of adorned elephants with palanquins transporting holy men coming into town, with great fanfare. There were fakirs lying on beds of nails or with bricks hanging from their testicles, snake charmers, brass bands, elegant costumes and a cacophony of chanting, wailing and spiritual razzamatazz filling the scene. It looked like a combination of Burning Man and Cirque de Soleil, on steroids! These colorful and spectacular scenes blew my mind, and I began to feel a palpable level of reverence and devotion for what had brought people here from all over the world.

It was quite something for this young man from South London, whose idea of a great night out was watching soccer on TV at a friend's house, getting stoned or going to the pub to get drunk—to arrive at this spiritual extravaganza.

I had been guided to leave England to find myself. I didn't know what that meant, but landing in the center of this massive devotional gathering quite by *chance*, had a huge impact on me. Amantane had told me that travelling would open my mind to the influence of different cultures and experiences. It felt like I had to have the biggest experience early on in my trip and have my mind blown open as I witnessed the vast difference in cultures. What I had always perceived about culture came from small-minded behaviors and beliefs, as I had lived a life quite constrained by English culture and its religious and political structures. My Catholic upbringing had not allowed me to question anything outside my normal frame of reference, which I believed was the one Truth.

I had lived in an area of South London where many Indians, Pakistanis and Bengalis also lived, so I was exposed peripherally to their foods and cultures. Due to peer pressure and cultural conditioning, I had also grown up with racist feelings towards them, even though I can't recall any incidences in which anyone did anything to me that warranted those feelings.

As is typical with racists, it was just my way of feeling better about myself—by putting down others from different cultures or traditions. Racism was not something that I learnt at home. As I got older, I started to question it and I recognized it was a behavior I didn't like about myself and resolved to eradicate it. It was very important to me as I embarked on my journey that I let go of any judgements and negativity towards people of other cultures and especially from countries with vastly different cultures and religions than my own. This was one of the reasons I chose India as my jumping off point. My racist views quickly changed, as I was treated with kindness and openness in India and the other Asian countries that I visited.

OPENING THE MIND

The message I was receiving during this seminal time in Haridwar was to open my mind—not just to see spirituality from a broader sense, but to also see the potential for my own life from a more expanded place. I was being given this incredible opportunity to experience devotion in a new way, by hanging out with Saddhus on the banks of the Ganges River and listening to their intriguing stories and hearing about their lives of abstinence. I felt like I had taken the *Red Pill* and stepped into a completely new and fascinating way of experiencing life. My reality was being completely shattered.

A MEETING ON A BRIDGE

Over years of travelling around the world, it was not the historical sites, or the beauty of nature that has touched my soul, but instead, it's the people I met along the way who affected me deeply. One such occasion early on in my trip I experienced a simple connection that has since stayed with me. I was walking on a very busy footbridge going over the Ganges River. I was still at the Kumbh Mela and throngs of people were on the move, which is typical for India. I saw in the distance a Caucasian guy wearing white robes, who was obviously a spiritual practitioner. As I drew closer, I could see by his hair cut that he was a Hare Krishna devotee.

We locked eyes and I knew this was going to be a meaningful interaction. I felt my whole body tingling and telling me it was important for me to talk to this man. We greeted each other with a smile of recognition and an unspoken knowing that we were meant to meet right here on this bridge.

David, I learned, was from the US. He had been a Hare Krishna practitioner for eight years. He was about my age. I was touched by his commitment to a life of devotion to a religion that wasn't part of his family history. It was one that I didn't understand but was eager to find out more. I had not been a practitioner of anything, although I felt I was now moving towards something.

We must have talked for 90 minutes on that bridge; we talked about our lives and our struggles. It was incredibly heartfelt, honest and real, as though we, two strangers on a bridge, were brought together just for this opportunity for clearing, sharing, and connecting.

I was being vulnerable. This wasn't something I was used to, coming from a family, culture, and religion in which I had never felt safe to open my heart like this. As we stood there chatting, people continued talking and walking around us as though we were invisible. It felt as though we were in a protective bubble of love and safety. It felt incredibly liberating to be able to share my feelings so easily with someone—both a friend and stranger: I wanted more of this!

MENTAL ILLNESS

I grew up in a culture in the United Kingdom that didn't honor psychotherapy as an important part of mental and emotional health. Going to a psychotherapist was considered taboo and in fact I didn't even know a therapist. I had never considered it an option. Today, I see that younger version of myself as having mental illness and someone who desperately needed professional help.

AMANTANE SPEAKS AGAIN

The sites and the people at the festival were incredibly photogenic, so I snapped away at the beautiful temples and colorful people whom I met. What a thrill I thought it would be for my family in England to see me standing in front of such amazing buildings and sitting next to the ash covered holy men. I was excited to see how my pictures looked, so I quickly had a few rolls developed in a local camera store.

I was struck by whom I saw looking back at me from my photos; it was the same unhappy guy who had left England a month before. The circumstances and the scenes in the background were very different to anything I had experienced up to that moment, yet the person looking back at me was still the same. So, was anything changing? I realized then that travel alone wasn't enough.

I remember feeling momentary panic. I had to do something else. But what? In that moment of deep questioning, Amantane spoke to me. **"You have to build your character. You have to build inner strength and learn to not believe the self-diminishing chatter that goes on inside your head."**

But how do I do that? I asked. *I don't know how!*

"You have already started. You left the safety net and comfort of what was familiar. But leaving is not all that is required. That may just be a form of running away from your problems. What you have to do is face your issues— fully, completely and trust yourself."

But how do I do that? I implored him.

As usual, Amantane responded immediately:

"You are going to find an Indian village, somewhere small and remote. You are going to live there for three months and try your best to immerse yourself in the culture, learn the language and get to know the people. Spend time with yourself: really with yourself. Look inside to see your gifts; the kinder, gentler parts of yourself. Recognize the beauty and the kindness that you hold in your heart. Learn to be grateful to yourself—your body, and your mind. You are a beautiful man. Live accordingly. Learn that your depression was a gift, an impulse to really start living. After all, if it wasn't for the depression, you wouldn't be experiencing the rich and rewarding experiences you are now having.

I will tell you—you have a bigger mission for your life."

For as long as I can remember I had been self-conscious. My life depended so much on what others thought of me. I often felt I was living for others more than I was living for myself. Maybe to experience this new form of isolation surrounded by people who had never met me, with whom I didn't have a history and who never formed an opinion of me, would be just what I needed? I felt as though I was being given a blank canvas to create a new way of living in any way I was willing. My life was mine to create. I didn't have to worry about what people thought of me as I was only going to stay in the village for three months. I could just be who I was for myself. I could learn about myself, explore myself—build myself in a fresh way, away from the neurotic attachments I had developed over the previous twenty-eight years of my life. I could birth myself anew. Holy shit—that sounded scary!

I trusted my guide, so off I went.

3

DEPRESSION—*my secret friend*

Hardships often prepare
Ordinary people
For an extraordinary destiny.

~ C.S LEWIS

My negative states of mind certainly weren't easy to live with and yet, I chose to live with them. I have to admit, I was attached to them by choice—after all, who else was making that choice? As difficult as it was to be inside my body and my mind, I felt *comfortable* within the familiarity of both of them.

My depression had in some delusionary way made me feel special. It was my secret; my unique experience that nobody else knew about. Now I was ready to let go of my highly critical but familiar inner *friend*, to find the higher and better version of myself. I was being guided to build my character, my inner resources and my spiritual strength.

My experiences in earlier life framed my view of reality and I often masked my pain through drug or alcohol use, or some other anesthetic. My fear of vulnerability kept me in a state of zombification—I was afraid to feel my feelings. I was unaware that those feelings were my body's way of pointing out where my attention needed to go. Ignoring them kept me in a perpetual state of self-destruction. My behaviors caused my body and mind to develop sicknesses and imbalances.

KONDABAL

While searching for the right village I met some locals who told me that Monsoon season was on the way and the best place to head was a state up north, like Himachel Pradesh or Kashmir, since that area would not be affected by daily heavy rain. I *serendipitously* met a Kashmiri guy on a bus who told me about a little village where he lived, located on the edge of a lake called Manasbal. He knew of a family who had a room for rent above their cattle shed that sounded perfect.

The curious family who owned the little room became my family for the next three months. We agreed on what I considered a very low price for the room, but to them was probably a small fortune. I also had a little side room that served as my kitchen, and the family provided me with a small gasoline stove and a couple of pots and plates as my only kitchen wares. Over the next few months, I cooked up some lavish meals on that little one-ring kerosene burner!

My humble room was situated on the edge of the beautiful lake: this lake also became my water supply, my kitchen sink and bath tub for my entire stay.

In this quaint village of Kondabal, time stood still. Here it seemed that nothing had changed for hundreds of years. The only indication of modern life was the occasional truck collecting flour—the main industry of the area. Electricity was sporadic and more often than not, my nights were lit with kerosene lamps.

I very quickly became the talk of the town. I couldn't walk through the village without having a procession of villagers following me and calling me *Sahib*. Sahib means *great man* and is a term of respect or honor given to important people, the same way *Don* is given in Spanish. I certainly didn't feel special, but nonetheless I became a celebrity because I was different and a curiosity for many. I felt like a White extra-terrestrial.

The sons of my landlord were learning English at school, so I was able to communicate with them and learn about their lives. They often spent time in my room carefully examining the meager contents of my backpack. With great attention, they would hold the items, turn them around in their hands and admire them like they were priceless Fabergé eggs. They marveled at anything that was made outside of India and they were eager to know the cost of my things. I enjoyed watching them imagine vicariously through the objects they held—a world outside of their little remote village.

Sometimes they would bring a friend or two to show them my simple possessions and recount in great detail where I had bought the individual pieces and how much I had paid for them. Their friends would sit there wide-eyed, fascinated by my treasures, such as my boots and sunglasses. They were all especially intrigued by my Sony Walkman!

I spent my days studying Kashmiri (the local language), paddling my Shikara (dugout canoe) on the lake and going for walks in the surrounding hills wearing native Kashmiri pajamas and Indian sandals. I was trying my best to integrate into this fascinating culture. I surprised myself by my willingness to live in such a completely different way. For me—it was off the charts!

I journaled daily—another completely new experience for me. I enjoyed processing my thoughts and writing about what was happening to me, including my personal encounters with locals. I knew it was important to develop deeper personal awareness and I reflected on these words from Amantane:

"Look inside to see your gifts: the kinder, gentler parts of yourself. Recognize the beauty and the kindness that you hold in your heart."

I had to learn how to be more loving to myself. I was not here to waste time and I resolved to write words of self-love, support and encouragement. At first this felt very uncomfortable but I stuck with it. I developed a daily routine of journaling, meditation and exercise, rowed my Shikara on the lake and cooked simple meals on my little stove. I continued my studies of Kashmiri with great enthusiasm.

Manasbal is a beautiful Muslim area with the majestic snow-covered Himalayas as its backdrop. Here I witnessed firsthand how an ancient Muslim village practiced its customs. Being here during Ramadan, the month of fasting, I experienced how devoted these villagers were in this time of abstinence—with bits of cheating going on!

One day I helped a few local women fetch clean water in large earthenware jars from the center of the lake. This was a common ritual that had been practiced for as long as their village existed. Helping them carry their heavy water jars was not customarily a man's role here and I was teased by both men and women for days afterwards. They found it highly amusing.

They also were amused by my attempts to communicate in their local language. Speaking Kashmiri with a London accent was met with quizzical looks so, I soon learnt to speak Kashmiri with an Indian accent. I still got friendly teasing, but at least they understood me better.

In my walks through the village, I began to feel a bit like the *Pied Piper* as throngs of villagers followed me through town.

Mothers would often hold their young children up to a window as I passed by and just utter one word—"Sahib".

Despite the attention I got whilst out and about, I still felt very alone and isolated. I realized that my loneliness was because of the emptiness I felt inside due to my self-rejection. This was the perfect time for me to really look at myself; after all, that's why I was here.

When I reflected on my circumstances in comparison to the villagers, I saw that I had so much freedom because I didn't have to work and my time in this village was only temporary. I was foot loose and fancy free! I started to look at what I had, rather than what I didn't have. I became aware that I had this blank canvas and I could design my life in any way I wanted. It felt like a re-birth.

Back home I had felt like a nobody—invisible and insignificant—yet here, in this remote Indian village I was Sahib—a great man. What was it like to feel like a great man? This was my work; it was time to own it and to honor the greatness in myself.

I decided I had to start living a non-ordinary life, an exceptional life, to really embody what I was being called: Sahib—great man. I decided to think in a new way and do what was required to make the big shift from meekness into greatness.

It was time for me to hold personal accountability and do whatever I had to do—to live from my heart and my strengths.

I was guided by Amantane to live for three months in this town. He knew it would be challenging for me but that was the point. At times I felt extremely lonely and out on a limb. The length of time was significant enough for me to change old habits and to start developing new ways of being and relating to myself. I knew this was a pivotal time for my growth, so I endured it. I now see it as one of the most important periods of my life.

DAVID BOWIE

I don't know where I'm going from here,
but I promise it won't be boring.

~ D.B.

Since my early teens I have been an avid fan of the music and personality known as David Bowie. (His real name was David Jones). Throughout his career he regularly developed alter egos in both his look and musical style, until his death from liver cancer in 2016.

Why am I writing about a rock-star in this book? Because Bowie's fearlessness and willingness to take chances were more important to him than to continue riding a wave of popularity based on previous successes. He took chances. He shapeshifted. He was passionate about life and his creativity.

What was paramount for him was to live his authentic life, even if that life was disguised behind the current alter ego which he presented to the world.

He inspired me and I too have changed my life in many ways and have taken chances, even when I didn't know where they would lead me. One could say that I too have alter egos, as the Alan I present to the world continues to be an evolution of the previous one.

LETTING GO OF
LIMITATIONS

Be a light unto yourself.
~ BUDDHA

I knew that I needed to let go of the conditioning and the limitations I had set for myself. I had to accept full responsibility for my current and future life which would not be defined by my past behaviors and belief systems. I would have to create this life from a completely new paradigm of thought, action and behavior.

Rather than continue blaming others—my parents, my schooling, my culture, and my religion—I began to develop a radical new way of looking at my life. I started to explore what actions I could take to really change the outcomes for my future, to not just live an ordinary life, but to live what I hoped would be an extraordinary life.

I started making a list for myself for how I could improve my mental states.

Notes to Self:

Acknowledge my successes.
Develop pride in my actions and decisions. Honor my victories, no matter how small. If I can change a little bit, I can change a lot.

Be curious.
Learn to examine cultures, religions, thoughts. Travel with an open mind and not make judgments about cultural norms that are different from my own. If I don't understand something— ask questions.

Be Decisive.
There is a big difference between impulsiveness and decisiveness even though to others my decisions may seem impulsive. For example, when I embarked on this trip, I did so with certainty. Others around me thought I was making a big mistake and being impetuous and impulsive but that view was based on their own fears around doing the same thing.

Build self-esteem.
Start believing in my greatness. Use kinder and more affirming words to myself.

Create clear and realistic goals.
If I set my goals too high it will lead to frustration, however it is also important I set goals that stretch my comfort level. Start to create goals that lift me up and allow me to thrive.

Get out of my comfort zone—often.
I resolve to try things that I have never tried before, because

in doing so I realize that what used to make me uncomfortable doesn't anymore.

Persevere.
Perseverance is the path to greatness and success. As Albert Einstein wrote, *"Life is like riding a bicycle. To keep your balance, you must keep moving."* As I continue to build my character and self-awareness, I will not allow negative states of mind to color my capacity to follow through.

Release Perfectionism.
Learn that it doesn't matter if something—an experience, a creation, an act—isn't perfect; it can still be damn good. Applying this way of thinking to others, I am also learning to let go of expectations and judgements of them and this is also making me happier.

Think Creatively.
I will be careful with what I wish for, what words I use and the thoughts I focus on to expand my way of thinking. I live in a benevolent Universe and what I put out into the Universe will come back to me.

Having the spaciousness to reflect and meditate on these targets was a vital part of my subtle life shifts. This time was about ME and for ME. It would have been hard to fit this process into my previously busy life.

Despite the fact that I was still having down days, I became aware that I was starting to feel more hopeful. I was in fact, doing something exceptional. I was doing something really different from anything I, or anyone I knew, had ever done.

So, here I was, in this small Indian Village, four months after leaving the UK, learning the local customs and communicating in their native language. But more importantly, I was letting go of limiting self-talk and moving away from intense self-hatred. I was creating new habits and letting go of old ones.

I did contract viral Hepatitis after two months in the village and lost twenty pounds in a month. I had no mirror, so I didn't notice my rapid weight loss, though I could tell I was yellow from head to foot. A house boat owner from Srinigar, the capital of Kashmir, whom I had stayed with before coming to Kondabal, came to visit me. When he saw me, he exclaimed—"You're going to Die!". I understood what the expression *mellow-yellow*, meant in that moment, as I reacted with calmness to his words and was unphased.

When I was able to look at myself in a full-length mirror, I could see why he was so shocked by my appearance. I looked extremely gaunt!

While staying with him on his houseboat, one month later, after my time in the village, he called in a spiritual healer to help me with my illness. This was my first experience ever with a *shaman*. That experience stayed with me and no doubt influenced my fascination with this mode of healing in recent years. To help my liver recover fully, I gave up drinking alcohol for five years straight.

I recovered quickly and carried on with my travels.

COMING HOME TO ME

In the Indian State of Himachel Pradesh, there sits a beautiful high mountain town called Manali. It was here that I was shown that there is more to life than I had previously realized, and I was given an introduction to a completely new way of understanding reality.

On the day I arrived in Manali, I entered a temple that was in the latter stages of construction. I observed the walls covered with the most amazing murals that I had ever seen. They were painted with a myriad of bright colors, depicting fantastical beings surrounded by Buddhas and angelic-looking deities. I was awestruck by the peaceful look on their faces. I had never seen such beautiful and diverse looking religious works of art. This was a stark contrast to the majority of Christian artwork I had seen in London art museums, as those were often single pointedly gory and bloody, with immense heaviness and suffering filling the canvases.

Here I stood in this place of worship, where serenity, peace and power were displayed together; I was filled with a sense of wonderment and awe.

I had stepped into what I soon learned was a Tibetan Buddhist Temple. Manali is a town with outlying communities of Tibetan refugees, who had been escaping the Chinese invasion of their homeland since 1950. They all followed the Fourteenth Dalai Lama who led the escape and who himself had settled in the mountain town of Dharamsala, not far from Manali.

As I crossed over the threshold of the temple doors, I simultaneously crossed over into a Life change. Upon entering the Sacred Space and seeing the artwork on the walls, I experienced a flood of intense emotions throughout my whole body. I had entered into a world that felt familiar. *What is this?* I questioned internally. *I know this.* It felt as though I had entered a time machine and had been transported back through lifetimes, to a place I had known before. I was transfixed. I didn't know what I was feeling or seeing but, I knew that I knew what it was. I stood there awestruck with waves of *knowing* flowing through me and a deep awareness of a Past life.

As I stood in the Temple, completely overwhelmed by my experience, I heard Amantane say, **"You have come Home!"**

Upon hearing his words, I felt a sense of inner peace; I now understood the deeper reason I had chosen to come to this part of the world. Amantane had not told me where I should go, just that I needed to travel the world for a period of time. I am the one who intuitively made the decision to come to Asia.

In a split second, as I entered the Tibetan Temple, I knew that I was meant to come here. It became clear that I was being directed through an intuitive awakening within myself, clearer than I had ever experienced before. *You have come home*, also meant a coming home to me and I was literally revisiting an ancestral home from a previous life.

Having been raised Catholic, this was a new reality for me. The idea that we have past lives—known as reincarnation—was not a part of my previous belief system. In Manali, I was experiencing an expansion of awareness beyond my conditioned mind.

What is this? What is happening? I asked myself.

I felt as though I was in an LSD journey similar to ones I had experienced a decade before. But this time, I had not taken any psychedelics and yet, I found myself transported by these paintings into a world of fantastic adventures.

The paintings, known as Thangkas, are specific to the form of Buddhism practiced in Tibet, known as Vajrayana. Many of the strange looking beings are known as Wrathful Deities, who destroy obstacles to the teaching and lessons taught by the more peaceful looking Buddhas. These Wrathful Deities represent the power that is required by humans to transform negative beliefs and mental states, into wisdom and awareness.

In that moment I received a download of this knowledge and it filled me with excitement!

On exiting the Temple and feeling quite shaken up, I saw a young Tibetan man standing with a small group of friends, looking at me and smiling. He broke away from his group and offered me an outstretched hand, introducing himself as Sonam Tashi. Sonam, it turned out, was one of the artists who had painted the amazing Thangkas.

Sonam, I asked: *Can you tell me about those paintings in there?*

He told me about his studies as an artist and about the intensive training that was required to become one. He then explained some of the meanings and philosophies in the artwork. Sonam went on to describe how the fearsome looking deities can destroy the underlying causes of suffering such as greed, hatred and delusion, through certain meditation practices. I liked what I was hearing.

Meeting him in that moment felt like a divine coincidence.

Where can I get one of these paintings? I asked him in earnest. I knew that I had to have some of this amazing artwork. Together we walked back to his little room near the temple, where he showed me some small paintings he had recently completed. I excitedly bought them on the spot. I then commissioned several large ones from a book of Thangka paintings he showed me. I had never commissioned a piece of art in my life, but I felt compelled to own more of these incredible Buddhist paintings.

It took Sonam many months to finish the works of art, and thirty-seven years later, they remain among my most prized possessions. They hung for years on the walls of my retreat center in California and they now adorn the walls of our new retreat center in Ecuador.

PAST LIVES

Collective memories of past experiences are embedded in our consciousness, as on a computer's hard drive. These are sometimes referred to as The Akashic Records and are recorded as a stream of experience, memories and past actions uninterrupted by physical death. A sense of this knowledge was revealed to me when I entered the portal to the Temple.

I was filled with excitement because I knew that there was much more to me than the reduced version of myself—the flesh and blood Alan—that I had always perceived. In that moment, I recognized there was a greater potential for my life than I had ever felt before. After this life changing experience, I was ready to go deeper on my journey into my-self.

COMPASSION IN ACTION—
Tibet

Only when compassion is present
Will people allow themselves
To see the truth.

~ GABOR MATÉ

Following six months in India, I spent four months in Nepal and then headed by road and on foot into Tibet. It was Tibet that had the greatest influence on me during my eighteen-month journey in Asia.

I was awestruck not just by the high altitude, the rawness and the harshness of Tibet's landscape, but by the demeanor, softness and kindness of the Tibetan people. The gentleness and grace of the Tibetan people stood in stark contrast to the harshness and arrogance of the Chinese invaders. The Chinese strutted around Tibet with an air of superiority as the great conquerors of the humble Tibetans.

Despite their deep philosophical and spiritual wisdom, the Tibetans appeared childlike in their countenances, smiling with boundless love in their compassionate eyes. I sensed a profound spiritual awareness in the elders' wrinkled and leathery faces. Just to look at them, and to witness them walking, prostrating, or sitting and praying using their 108 beaded *Malas* (like a Christian rosary), was humbling and heart opening for me.

Their spiritual leader, the fourteenth Dalai Lama, had been living in exile in India since he escaped from the Chinese invasion in 1959 at the age of 23.

A fellow traveler who had just visited Tibet, advised me to bring photos of the Dalai Lama to give to Tibetans. He warned me to do this in secrecy, as to own a photo of His Holiness could mean a long prison sentence to a Tibetan. I carefully handed out several of these photos to locals with whom I connected, who responded with so much love and adoration in their faces—it often brought tears to my eyes.

WALKING IN REVERENCE

Barkhor Square is the central market square in Lhasa, the capital city of Tibet. It is also the area that houses one of the most sacred and revered temples in the whole of Buddhism: the 1300-year-old Jokhang Temple. The Jokhang houses a unique and highly treasured statue of Jowo Shakyamuni (Buddha)—which is said to have been carved in the Buddha's lifetime over 2500 years ago.

Tibetans typically walk meditatively and with great respect, around all temples. They always walk in a clockwise direction; the direction in which they believe they can find wisdom and compassion to purify negative karma. It is done as an act of devotion and respect for their beliefs and traditions.

The Chinese invaders, as a show of power and moral authority, make a point of walking counterclockwise, against the flow—to impress on the Tibetans how ignorant and unimportant their rituals are to them. They look down on them as though they are less than animals. I imagined that the gentle Tibetans use this as a forgiveness opportunity to share compassion with their captors. Their display of compassion became a beautiful lesson for me in practicing *metta*, or loving kindness. I don't feel I was as good at it as the Tibetans because I felt angry and upset by the how the Chinese treated these gentle people.

I felt profound sadness learning of the brutal invasion by the Chinese People's Army, with the genocidal and harsh treatment they continue to inflict upon the Tibetan people.

While traveling in the areas where tourists were allowed, I saw the senseless destruction of temples littering the high desert landscape. Around ten thousand temples overall had been ruthlessly destroyed. It was a devastating scene that left me questioning man's inhumanity to one another.

Since that time, I now tend to walk in a clockwise direction around important buildings such as shrines and museums, and in nature, etc. I do it to honor the Tibetan people. I also find it a simple, beautiful ritual and beneficial practice of mindfulness.

I began thinking deeply about what I was witnessing in Tibet. How was it that these kind Tibetans appeared so happy with so little and yet, many from my culture—who have so much in comparison, are so unhappy?

It was becoming clear to me, that the practice of compassion and loving kindness is a real thing and a powerful path that leads one out of depression and other negative states.

THE HEART OPENS IN TIBET

Something significant was happening to me in Tibet. My heart opened to the Tibetans and in my heart opening to them, my heart opened to me. I began to soften to myself. I realized that in witnessing their gentleness and kindness, I was inspired to become gentler and kinder towards myself.

In Tibet I learnt more about Buddhist practices, and I started to understand the deeper meaning behind *actions have consequences*, the first teaching I had received from Amantane. I realized that all my actions would have subsequent reactions, whether intended or not. If I wanted to continue on my path of exploring happy states, this would mean paying attention to my beliefs, thoughts and behaviors.

I was walking on a path of wisdom and without knowing it I was embarking on my apprenticeship as a healer!

BUDDHISM

One of the great gifts that traveling offered me was the opportunity to witness and observe the behaviors and demeanors of people from other cultures. In India specifically, as I traveled from state to state, I could immediately sense a difference in people's attitudes and actions.

The majority of Indian states are Hindu, but there are also states that are primarily Muslim, Buddhist or Christian. I observed that religious influences affected personalities and behavioral characteristics. I found the Muslims to be quite serious and disciplined, the Hindus very playful, boisterous and colorful, and the Buddhists to be calm, gentle and friendly. With no disrespect meant to any religion, I became naturally inclined towards the Buddhist character and practices. I felt that my experience at the temple in Manali where I had my past-life flashback, was a significant factor in this inclination.

Buddhism is a fundamentally simple path within its complex teachings. It's an aware path and within that awareness lies the keys to mental and emotional liberation from suffering. It is also a path of vigilance and mindfulness, as the human mind has a natural proclivity towards negativity, and that negativity can pounce on you like a fire breathing dragon.

RESISTING MANIPULATION AND HATRED

For a short time during my journey, I travelled with a couple of German guys who were about my age: Oliver and Johann. It was the first time in my life that I'd spent an extended period of time getting to know any Germans. I became quite close to Oliver and Johann and liked them a lot. One of our most impactful conversations centered around Hitler and the Nazis during World War II.

I wondered how people like them—friendly, intelligent, caring, and warm—could come from a country that had been involved in such atrocities and intense hatred—which had caused such deep suffering. How could regular Germans like my friends have been so manipulated to kill their neighbors and friends?

I also examined my own country of birth—England and its history in achieving world dominance and how so many of my forefathers had also been manipulated in the name of patriotism and tribal fealty. I also reflected on my own earlier proclivity towards racism.

I asked myself, if I had been a young man in Germany during the period of widespread manipulation and brainwashing, would I have had the strength of character to resist the coercion techniques used by the Nazi party?

I honestly couldn't answer Yes—I didn't know if I would have had the strength or mental discipline to resist the political and peer pressure. I felt so deeply troubled by my lack of conviction that I decided in that moment I would do whatever it took to grow and strengthen my character. I wanted to be sure that in the future I would never allow myself to be brainwashed and manipulated to do or think abhorrent, unethical, immoral things towards anyone, no matter their race, religion or culture.

RETURNING TO ENGLAND

A ship in harbor is safe,
But that is not
What ships are built for.

~ JOHN A. SHEDD

I had been on the road in Asia for eighteen months before finally heading back to the UK. Initially, I had been very nervous about embarking on my Asia journey, as it was so different from anything I had ever done before. It turned out that I was more nervous about going back into the familiar—back to the mundane and myopic life I had lived in South London.

My journey had been so extraordinary. I had experienced so many incredible cultures, seen beautiful vistas, met so many open-minded people and now I felt such trepidation. I didn't know how I would manage back in my homeland. What would my friends and family think about me now? Would they consider me a freak because of my new views about life? More than anything, I was worried about being back in my old and familiar sphere of influence, which might cause me to regress into my previous depressive states—which I was happily no longer experiencing.

The most surprising and disappointing element of being back in England was that virtually *no one* asked me about my travels! I had been gone for a year and a half and had experienced the most incredible adventures and yet no one in my network, including my family, showed any interest in any of it. It was like I had never left, as though time just stood still. The conversations were exactly the same as before and I was utterly confused and dumbfounded! There was a blatant lack of curiosity which felt so alien to me now. Once I got over my initial disappointment, I made the decision to continue living what I knew I wanted—an extraordinary life filled with travel, curiosity and adventure.

Despite my increased self-awareness, my concerns about re-experiencing my old negative mind spaces were justified. Quite quickly, I started to feel heavier and less happy being back in this environment. Being back here triggered my old patterns. I did not, however, fall back into depression. I had thankfully developed the awareness that I was sovereign over the choices I made and the thoughts that I allowed. I did recognize however, that the family baggage I had carried for so long was still there.

I was now aware that I had to take any actions necessary that would continue to support the changes I had made in my life, so I started to look for new friends who were open-minded, who had curiosity and who were also critical thinkers. Fortunately, I found some.

I began making my living as an antique dealer at the famous London markets, Portobello Road and Camden, where I sold crafts that I had imported from Asia and collectibles that I bought at auctions around England. I mixed with a new type of Londoner who seemed more curious and independent, and who also earned a living in a fringe way, because we didn't want to be working for *the Man*. To my good fortune, these new friends were very interested in my travels and the path that I had taken to actively change my mental states.

I joined a Buddhist group and voraciously read books on Buddhist philosophy. I visited countries in Europe where I had never travelled to before: Portugal, Spain and Turkey. All the while I was saving money so I could embark on another extended journey, this time to explore South America!

TRAVELS IN SOUTH AMERICA

Travel isn't always pretty.
It isn't always comfortable. Sometimes it hurts,
It even breaks your heart.
But that's okay. The journey changes you; it should change you.
You take something with you.
Hopefully, you leave something good behind.

~ ANTHONY BOURDAIN

My way of life changed dramatically following my journey around Asia. It became clear to me that I had to permanently leave the country of my birth. I loved the sense of freedom and the variety of experiences I had traveling around the developing world, more than I liked my life in England.

I felt I was sort of an amateur anthropologist, fascinated by ancient cultures and their religious and spiritual traditions. I loved the temples of India, Nepal and Tibet. I loved the people of these countries. I was enamored with their pageantry and religious devotion. I was awestruck and inspired by the religious practices of the Balinese Hindus, with their daily processions of flower and fruit offerings in breathtakingly beautiful temples. I fell in love with the Elephant God, Ganesha—known for removing obstacles. His statues always stood front and center of the main entrances—blocking the way so you had to avoid the obstacle he symbolically represented.

After my journey to Asia, I was hooked on travel. I became a man with a mission. I spent a year back in the UK, working two, sometimes three jobs, to save money for my new way of life. I worked very hard so I could take off for a solid twelve months, allowing me to travel for a year, uninterrupted. I set off on a twelve-month exploration of South America.

LEARNING THE LINGO

Landing in Lima, Peru, knowing hardly a word of Spanish, I learned the word *vegetariano* very quickly—for all the good that did me. Back then, in the late 1980's, South Americans didn't understand the concept of vegetarian; it was a land of meat and chicken eaters. I ended up eating huevos y arroz (eggs and rice) for a greater part of my time there; sometimes if I was lucky, I got a potato or carrot on my plate. Often the dish would be brought to my table with chunks of chicken in the rice or a dollop of gravy over the eggs. "Well, just take out the chicken or scrape off the gravy," the waiter would say. I soon learnt the phrase *"Si como carne, me muero!"*: If I eat meat, I die! That worked most of the time!

Initially, I spent extended periods of time on my own because I didn't know the language. This motivated me to learn Spanish quickly. I soon discovered speaking decent Spanish in Peru made a huge difference in my experience. I would sometimes even get invited into people's homes.

I was fascinated by what I learnt of the best-known ancient culture of South America, the Incas. These powerful people were almost completely wiped out by the Spanish conquistadors following their arrival in 1532. I visited Machu Pichu, the most famous Incan Citadel, otherwise known as The Crystal City, that had been *lost to civilization* until 1911 when it was *rediscovered* by North American anthropologist Hiram Bingham. This was one of the important Incan sites that had not been conquered by the Spanish invaders, as it was built on top of a mountain and out of sight—which is part of its mystery.

Little did I know then, how some of the Incan traditions would play such a big part in my life in less than a decade.

I was visiting Peru at a time of great disruption as a Marxist Terrorist Group was wreaking havoc around the country. Known as Sendero Luminoso (Shining Path), their aim was to overthrow the democratically elected government and install a communist dictatorship through guerrilla warfare. I had read about the dangers of going to Peru due to all the violence and murders that were common in those days and had read warnings about not going to areas where the Shining Path had control. I took those warnings seriously.

A side effect of the terrorist threats was that there were very few foreigners travelling. Sacred sites such as Macchu Picchu had few visitors, allowing those who did brave the journey—such as myself—to have these sites pretty much to ourselves. There were probably no more than twenty visitors the day that I visited. It's a very different story these days, as Macchu Picchu is today the most popular tourist site in the Americas.

SITTING WITH THE DYING

I never intended to end up in San Francisco, California.

After a year of traveling around South America, I was down to five hundred dollars in my pocket. Several North Americans whom I had met suggested I go to the San Francisco Bay Area and work *under the table* for a while, to earn some dollars. I had just enough money for a flight from Medellin, Colombia, to San Francisco, so off I went!

My plan was to stop in California briefly to earn money, then continue travelling in Latin America. Afterwards I planned to go back to Europe to live in Spain or Portugal. As good fortune would have it, I ended up staying in San Francisco for 25 years living in the beautiful City by the Bay.

When I first arrived, I didn't know anybody, but very quickly I found a job working in construction (fortunately I was very handy). I also started building friendships in the Castro District within the gay community.

My first boss, Ron Lanza, was a well-known pillar of this community. He opened a gay cabaret club/vegetarian restaurant, pretty soon after I arrived and is where I ended up helping with the construction. He named it after his Italian Grandmother—*Josie's Cabaret and Juice Joint*. Ron soon became my best friend and landlord.

Although I am not gay, I enjoyed being introduced to the lifestyles and parties of my gay friends in this very homosexual-centric area of the city. Unfortunately, in the early 1990's in San Francisco, the gay community was getting decimated by the AIDS virus. Most of my friends either had AIDS, or had lost many of their friends or lovers to this horrific virus.

I was keen to give back to the city and the community that had welcomed me so warmly, so I decided to reciprocate in the best way I could. I trained as a hospice volunteer with the Zen Hospice Project (ZHP) and started what would become a twenty-year spell as a bedside volunteer within that amazing organization. The ZHP was founded by Martha de Barros, Frank Ostaseski and other members of the Zen Buddhist Community in 1986, to help alleviate suffering at this critical time.

Sitting at the bedside of the dying became a big test of any fear I had of mortality, especially as the majority of patients were young men in their twenties and thirties. It was heartbreaking to see so many young lives terminated so swiftly. Sadly, this was the period before researchers understood that protease inhibitors—drugs that slowed the virus's replication process—could keep people alive, sometimes for years after infection. Thankfully, this soon became a successful treatment and catching the virus was no longer an automatic death sentence for millions of people.

LEARNING TO PROTECT MY ENERGY

Being an empath, I would sometimes feel very tired and energetically depleted sitting by the bedside of certain patients. After a while, I recognized that my energy was being drained by these patients—who could be seen as *energy vampires*. This didn't worry me as my energy would re-build once I left their bedside, but I knew that to continue working as a hospice volunteer, I would have to learn how to protect my energy. Otherwise, I would have to give up my work there—which I was incredibly passionate about.

Due to my Buddhist training, I knew there was a difference between empathy and compassion, so I decided to put my Buddhist practice to good use by exploring more deeply, how to move away from a state of empathy and into a state of compassion. An aspect of compassion is that one does not take on another person's energy.

My reason for wanting to do hospice work was not completely altruistic. I knew from the central Buddhist teaching, that the path that leads from suffering is the practice of both wisdom and compassion. There is nothing wrong with seeking compassion for yourself or showing kindness to others because it makes you feel good. We all have to start somewhere. At some point, the hope was that my actions would become altruistic: no longer about myself but about the other.

One of the greatest gifts I received from sitting at the bedside of the dying was learning about people's energetic needs. Every one of the hospice patients in that twenty-six-bed ward had different needs and requirements. Some needed help eating, some needed their bed and diaper changed, some needed hand-holding, some wanted special food brought in, some wanted company, some wanted me to sit quietly as they died, and others just wanted me to "Go the Hell Away!" I learned to read the energy around each person and not to just jump in and assume they wanted the same thing as the person in the bed on either side of them. This discernment was great training for me and a skill that has served both me and my healing clients.

Two decades of hospice volunteering has given me the ability to really sit with people who are undergoing deep suffering—without judgement. To be truly present and to deeply listen are great gifts to be able to offer to anyone. It was very heart opening for me to look another human being directly in the eyes. Opening the heart is the first step in moving away from suffering. Whatever the ailment, it is a source of great wisdom, and the greater the level of suffering, the deeper the fount of wisdom.

Learning how to protect my energetic space during my hospice work led me to training in Shamanic practices. This was beyond the spontaneous shamanic journeying I already had a lot of experience with since the age of 17, thanks to LSD.

ACID INDUCED JOURNEYS

I was introduced to Lysergic Acid Diethylamide, otherwise known as LSD or Acid, in my teens. LSD is a manufactured drug that can bring about hallucinogenic, or psychedelic experiences, and it was used during the 1960's counterculture movement to aid the expansion of consciousness. Some of the effects of LSD include the intensification of thoughts, emotions, and sensory perceptions.

For me and my friends, it was something to do on weekends to have *an experience* and to really feel and relate to the incredible psychedelic visions that music groups such as Pink Floyd would create for us. This music seemed perfect for the Acid trips we embarked on. Initially, I went into those experiences with no intention other than to get wasted, or to absentmindedly escape my everyday reality; I never realized how those experiences would shape my view of what reality was, as those journeys eventually built on each other.

For the first seventeen years of my life, I had been engaged with the world in the way that I had been conditioned to believe was the truth. Now, with the ingestion of this *truth serum*, I was experiencing a vast and expanded view of conscious reality, as though a door to the limitless nature of mind had opened. I was fascinated and intrigued. I started to see that the religious dogma I had been drip-fed my whole life was not true, that it had been misappropriated and misaligned by religious leaders—not always for the highest good.

From this point on, I began to distrust media news and the common narrative. I became an independent and critical thinker and could see more clearly how those in power were brainwashing the masses. I started to develop my highly sensitive bullshit meter. I became confused, I became rebellious, and I went deeper into my inner conflict—which was not a happy place.

At the age of 22, I realized these regular psychedelic experiences were sending me into a place of psychosis and paranoia. Because I was emotionally fragile, I was unable to handle the cumulative effects of such profound and intense journeys and I became more insular and disassociated. I decided to never take a psychedelic substance again—what a laugh considering how my life has unfolded!

My acid induced experiences did leave me with something unusual: I learnt that I could access non-ordinary states of consciousness *at will*. These allowed me to enter an expanded state of awareness, during which I was flying through the universe to imaginary worlds of animals and fantastical beings. These could shape-shift into anthropomorphic forms which possessed exceptional powers and insight. I could travel to planets and galaxies, flying free through space in non-embodied form.

I learnt how to enter these states regularly without LSD. I would tense my body, squeeze my eyebrows and lids tight, hold my breath, and will myself to enter this imaginary world, as though squeezing through a portal. Once I entered this state of cosmic travel, I could just let go, lie back and relax. I would watch my mind go off on a journey that would guide itself outside of any thought or willed influence. I have no idea how long I would go on these interstellar explorations but I could bring myself out any time I chose.

But more than this, I felt like I was developing a new relationship to God. God was no longer just an abstract form of something powerful and Holy, to whom I prayed and whose existence I had not been allowed to question. Now, I was not just experiencing some archetypal subjective reality, I was connecting to a Divine Oneness of which I was part of the One. I seemed to be journeying into a collective consciousness of the creative intelligence of the universe. God was all around; God was everything—a unified field of awareness.

I was only 19 when I started doing this. I couldn't grasp the value and power of these transcendent and mystical experiences, but it was an important part of my journey that has continued to guide me and inform my view of truth. I became more and more familiar with the exalted states I entered through the portal of my imaginal experiences.

Being someone who had never learned to speak openly about my feelings or anything else of a personal nature, I kept these journeys and experiences to myself. I thought they were normal and this was just a common experience of growing up; I assumed I was just meditating.

I felt very light and free in my body and my mind, and I could fully relax and expand my thoughts in that state, which was a far cry from the usual tense and limited patterns and beliefs of my normal waking hours. It wasn't until about fifteen years later that I found out that what I was experiencing was not considered meditation. It had another name: it was called *Shamanic Journeying*!

DISCLAIMER

I am not an Allopathic Medical Doctor and
I do not make any claims about what health conditions
drinking Ayahuasca will heal. You the reader, are responsible
for making your own choices of what healing process
you entrust your body to and decide to follow.

PART II

The Alchemy of Ayahuasca

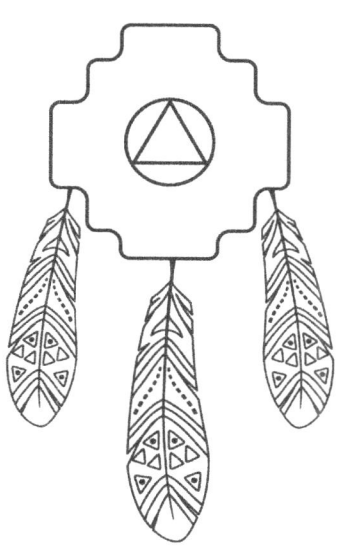

Alchemy is a medieval forerunner to modern science, most famously known for the quest of the transmutation of base metals into gold or, to render a universal cure for disease. This could also be seen as a metaphor for the self-realization of human consciousness or, the pursuit of inner transformation through the search for spirit in matter.

As they were working secretly to discover the Sacred Elixir, little did the medieval European alchemists know, that thousands of miles away in the deep jungles of unknown lands, indigenous botanists had already discovered the *pot of gold* they were searching for, which contained chemicals and alkaloids, not to be found in other parts of the world.

This elixir is commonly known today, as Ayahuasca—The Vine of the Soul.

The Ayahuasca brew, known as *Grandmother* or *Abuela*, is a combination of different plants from the Amazon rainforest that together bring about a transmutation of sickness into well-being through a spiritual and physical synergy.

The truly mysterious side to Ayahuasca's healing power is its spiritual component. She is a Master Plant Teacher as opposed to a plant medicine such as herbal remedies. She heals through spiritual intervention, as well as, through the chemical constituents in the combination of plants themselves. How that happens and what effects that will have on anyone drinking this magical brew is now and probably will forever, remain a mystery.

One could see the alchemical magic of the sacred brew as a synergy between Heaven and Earth, with the Ayahuasca vine bringing you into sacred relationship with Pachamama and all her relations and the DMT in the Chakruna leaf, metaphorically taking you to meet God.

I recommend reading: *DMT: The Spirit Molecule: A Doctor's Revolutionary Research into the Biology of Near-Death and Mystical Experiences* by Dr. Richard Strassman to learn more.

This section of the book is not meant as a definitive overview of the process of healing with Ayahuasca and does not cite any scientific evidence to back up my personal experiences. These reflections are from my spiritual journey with Ayahuasca that I began in earnest about eighteen years ago, when She very quickly instructed me to embark on an apprenticeship with Her. Today, I still continue on my apprenticeship of healing with the guidance of Ayahuasca, as She remains a powerful spiritual ally, both in and out of ceremony.

On the following pages I use the terms *She*, *Abuela*, or *Grandmother*, as honorific terms to denote that Ayahuasca is generally seen as a highly evolved female spiritual being, and who often appears as a green female form during ceremony. Sometimes She appears as a giant serpent.

If you make the decision to drink Ayahuasca, I recommend you only do so under expert supervision by someone you trust. Treat it as an opportunity to change aspects of your life that you have not been able to change up to this point.

You are your own best medicine.
Make clear choices.
Set clear boundaries.
Be extraordinary.

8

MY INTRODUCTION

There are all kinds of ways to challenge ourselves.
Some people do it by climbing a mountain or scuba diving.
The most prcfound and challenging ordeal
Is to drink Ayahuasca.
It is in a way the ultimate adventure.
~ GRAHAM HANCOCK

It was 2005 and I was living in Cusco, Peru, with my former wife Ursula. We had met in San Francisco in 1990, the year of my arrival there and we both loved to travel. As such, we decided to take a six-month break from our jobs and head to Peru. We moved down to the former capital of the Incan Empire to experience South American life: to do volunteer work, study Spanish and immerse ourselves as best we could in the Peruvian culture.

Because of my interest in hospice work, I found a volunteer position in an old folks' home that was run by an order of Catholic nuns. This was the closest to a hospice that I could find and it allowed me to share skills that I had developed with the Zen Hospice Project. Ursula found a job in a home for children with severe physical disabilities, also run by an order of Catholic Nuns (you gotta love the Catholic Nuns!)

Before leaving for our Peruvian adventure, I suddenly developed tinnitus: a loud ringing in my left ear, that I attributed to noise trauma caused by all the power tools in my woodworking shop. It was freaking me out and felt like torture. It didn't allow me a single moment of peace as the constant ringing filled my whole head with incessant noise.

I decided it was time for me to try Ayahuasca; I had heard about it in shamanic circles I was attending in San Francisco, so I decided to search out a local shaman to see if he could help me with my distressing malady.

I enjoyed walking the narrow cobblestone streets of Cusco and checking out the various shops and markets filled with indigenous textiles and sweaters made from Alpaca and Llama wool. I would come across flyers advertising Ayahuasca ceremonies, and even spoke to some shamans, but the few people I met didn't seem like they were the right ones to trust to take me on this big adventure. They had an air of arrogance about them. My bullshit meter has always been a good guide for me to discern whether or not to trust someone with my physical and spiritual well-being. From the little I had read about Ayahuasca, I knew that finding the right shaman was vitally important; this was a potentially powerful opportunity for a life change and I knew I should not make this decision lightly.

The San Pedro market in Cusco was where I bought herbal remedies and I often bought from an herbalist named Vicky. During one visit, I asked if she knew of any trustworthy Shamans and she told me she knew of a *Curandero* (healer) who was a well-respected *Ayahuasquero* (person who facilitates Ayahuasca ceremonies). I felt both excited and nervous at the thought of experiencing this powerful medicine.

On a rainy Saturday evening, I went with Vicky and her brother Mateo to a somewhat dubious part of town to meet the man Vicky had spoken highly of. We found him sitting in what appeared to be an old, small cattle shed made from adobe mud bricks. The walls and ceiling were covered with blue tarpaulin to keep the rain out, which was only moderately effective. The floor was covered with cheap mattresses and each mattress had a small empty yogurt carton beside it. These I assumed were for the purging (vomiting) I had heard was an integral part of the ceremonies.

After a brief introduction, Vicky and Mateo left me alone with the Shaman, who introduced himself as Maestro Pedro. He was a pleasant looking fellow with short hair and a stocky build. He looked about 45 years old. Although I didn't show it, I felt nervous about being there. I was sitting in this little hut with someone I had never met before and entrusting him to guide me on a deep dive into my inner world. What little that I had read about these journeys was not comforting at all. I had not met anyone firsthand who had experienced an Ayahuasca journey, so all of my information was from the internet.

The information described terrifying images of snakes and dragons infiltrating your mind and you can spend hours wallowing in the muck of your deeply held fears and limiting beliefs—things that you have kept buried in the depths of your subconscious. In addition, the ceremonies can include hours of vomiting, tears and diarrhea!

Maestro Pedro put any fears I had to rest, with his pleasant but matter-of-fact manner.

We talked for an hour—just me and him in the little hut, chatting about *Rocky films* and about how he had left the military and then trained for five years in shamanic work in the rainforests of Peru. He explained that Ayahuasca was the combination of two plants, Chakruna and Ayahuasca, that were brewed together for several hours. I was fascinated to learn that thousands of years ago, *someone* was divinely guided to choose these two plants out of over 100,000 plants in the Amazon jungle. S/He then macerated and mixed them together, boiled them for eight hours and for some reason, then drank the foul-tasting liquid! That in itself boggles the mind. What is more fascinating is the fact that many other tribes in Amazonia, were also using the same combination of plant mixtures, even though they had no contact with each other. That is even more mind boggling!

Ayahuasca has been used for thousands of years in the Amazonian region of South America as a healing herb for mental, emotional and physical conditions. Its use can also reveal to the Shaman other specific plants that can be administered to patients to help heal underlying conditions. In his description of the sacred brew, Maestro Pedro made it sound fascinating and I eagerly looked forward to the start of the ceremony.

The old adobe building where the ceremony was taking place had no windows and just an old creaky door. The night was filled with the sounds of thunder and lightning, with torrential rain crashing onto the tin roof, making the sound of rapid drumming. Maestro Pedro commented that the heavy rain must be what was keeping people away, as it was nearly time for the ceremony and it was still just the two of us.

He got up and came over to me holding a massive pipe filled with what he explained was jungle tobacco, known as *Mapacho*. Jungle tobacco, as I later found out, is considered one of the most powerful healing plants amongst the cornucopia of all the thousands of Amazonian plant species. It is blown via a pipe or a cigarette, to spiritually cleanse or purify the participants in the ceremony.

He first blew the tobacco smoke over my crown *chakra* at the top of my head and waited to see the formations the smoke created there. He explained that he was also looking for how quickly the smoke dispersed, to guide him to determine the level of my spiritual condition that would indicate to him my spiritual strength, to help him with my healing.

Then he blew the smoke towards the roof, or more accurately, the sky. Immediately, the heavy rain that had been pounding down for the last two hours—stopped. He looked at me with a glint in his eye and said, "It doesn't always work, but it worked this time!"

I was suitably impressed.

With the break in the rain, a couple of local people showed up to join us and we were ready to start the ceremony. Maestro Pedro explained to us that we were not allowed to leave the space, and with no bathroom, it was evident that the yogurt carton would be our vessel to contain any evacuation that was expelled from our bodies that night. With stories of diarrhea in my head—this promised to be an interesting ride! When I discovered the *toilet* the next morning, the yogurt carton somehow seemed like a better option!

We were each given a small cup full of a dark brew that smelled similar to molasses. I drank mine and cringed a little at the bitter taste. Maestro Pedro was the last to drink.

Little did I know just how familiar I would become with that taste over the coming years.

The other two participants and I looked each other in the eyes and smiled as a sign of support. Then it was lights off and the room went quiet. After about thirty minutes, Pedro started singing a song that began generating visions of beautiful sacred geometry inside my head, patterns of indescribable beauty in what seemed like a limitless expanse of consciousness. It didn't make any sense or have any meaning for me at the time, though it was described later to me, that the swirling spirals I saw could represent the double helix of my own DNA.

I was experiencing myself at a cellular level. The visions were there whether I had my eyes open or closed. I felt that I was experiencing the chemical structure of my cells and the Fibonacci spirals of sacred geometry represented the mystery of life itself. It was mind-blowing! I felt no fear, so I dove deeper into the visions, the intensity of which was somehow guided by the driving force of Pedro's sacred medicine songs.

At one point, the dancing geometry changed into a vision of myself standing at the edge of a cliff. More so, it felt like I was standing on the edge of the Universe. I knew intuitively I was witnessing the vastness of limitless consciousness and I was a composite part of what I was seeing. In a flash, I could sense the omnipresence of the creator of everything: God: Source Energy: Creation. The power and the massiveness of this made me feel completely insignificant. It was too big to comprehend: the sense of wisdom and knowledge held there was just too vast for little me! I couldn't take it all in at that moment: my ego could not grasp how huge the reality of what I was being shown actually was. Even though I felt so insignificant in that moment, I knew I was part of it all. I had to step back from the vision: it was too big for my mind to absorb in this first journey, so I chose to let it go. I would have to come back at a future time when I could understand it better and allow myself to jump off the edge—into the void.

My body went into convulsions and I started to purge and vomit into my tiny yogurt carton. Although I felt physically sick, I simultaneously felt gratitude knowing I was ejecting some form of toxicity from my body, mind or emotions. I heaved and projectile vomited on and off throughout the rest of the night. I had visions of myself as an Anaconda snake and saw that in order to regurgitate my own detritus, I had to dislocate my jaw to release the power, intensity and quantity of the deep purging.

I shape-shifted into many animals: a cow, a jaguar, a frog, a snake, a bat and a monkey, as though I was being shown just how much I was part of the natural world—to understand at a visceral level, how it was to be part of the animal kingdom—that I—a human—was also an animal.

At some point, Pedro called me over to lie down in front of him. I could only make out where he was by the red glow when he drew on his massive pipe. Somehow, I made it to him by crawling four feet to where he was sitting in the dark behind his altar.

"Quieres aumentar la medicina, Alan?" He asked (Do you want more medicine, Alan?). The second glass tasted even fouler than the first and I gagged on it.

Pedro instructed me to lie in front of his altar.

It's always important to go into an Ayahuasca ceremony—or any healing session for that matter—with a clear intention for the healing or outcome of the ceremony. In our pre-ceremony conversation, I had shared about my tinnitus with Pedro and I had developed a clear intention for him to help heal it.

Now, he told me to lie on my right side to allow him easy access to my left ear. He then started spraying perfumed flower water, blowing smoke into my ear and hitting me softly around the head and face with a rattle made of bunched *Chacappa* leaves. These leaves have a special vibration that help to move stuck energy. It sounded like a flock of birds flapping their wings all around me, giving me the impression that I was flying with them, outside of time and space. The fact that we were in a pitch-black room, intensified these feelings. It all felt so surreal.

"Concentrate" he said. "I am going to sing you a very powerful *Icaros* (sacred medicine song)."

I was ready. I felt strong and excited to go deeper into the connection with the snake and with nature. I was even more excited at the anticipation of this Maestro healing my tinnitus.

As Maestro Pedro started singing to me, I immediately became an Anaconda wrapping itself around the tree of life somewhere in the deep jungle. The level of my connection to the earth was deeper than I had ever experienced in my life, as the snake coiled itself around me and at the same time, I felt wrapped in this primal connection to not just this life, but to life itself. As Pedro sang for me, and to me, I became part of the pulse of nature, with Anaconda as Mother Earth, slithering and coiling around my humanity.

Ayahuasca was scanning me. She scanned my entire body, moving stealthily through me like a slithering snake. I found out later that the snake is also considered the spirit of the vine and is a common visitor.

As Pedro continued singing, a vision of a little man in my inner ear appeared. I could see him as though he was really there. He was sweeping the dusty floor in a little room inside of my ear. He was sweeping around the damaged hair follicles inside my inner ear to help cleanse the cause of the damage. Pedro sang with more intensity and blew more tobacco smoke into my ear, I felt myself go even deeper into the awareness of the vision, as I focused.

"Concentrate" he repeated. "Stay with the visions."

Suddenly the singing and rattling stopped and I felt the warmth of his breath close to my ear. Pedro started sucking from my ear. I felt he was trying to suck out the spiritual and energetic cause of the damage. All the while the little guy in my ear kept sweeping. Pedro sucked and spat for what seemed like fifteen minutes and then he gave a big purge into a bucket. He said I was done for today, but I needed to come back five more times!

Interestingly, I received in that moment the awareness that my tinnitus would not be healed, but that my life would be forever changed.

I sat up and immediately vomited into my yogurt carton. I felt like the purge came from the very depths of my soul and was cleansing every cell of my body. This was like no trip to the doctor's office! It was intense; it was beautiful and simultaneously bizarre and surreal.

How could I even explain this to anyone? How could I explain it to Ursula, who didn't even know if I would come back alive? This was like nothing I had ever experienced before in all my forty years but, I knew I was in excellent hands and despite Pedro's shack being in a sketchy part of Cusco, I felt very safe.

At this point I became aware of the other two participants, also going through their own process and vomiting and moaning. The energy felt so thick, it held the intensity of an otherworldly density.

I crawled back to my mat and things started to calm down. The extra glass of Aya took me into memories of my earlier life. Gently, She showed me events in my life that were the cause of my negative behaviors. I saw how my distant relationship to a father whom I didn't like or respect—had framed my view of manhood. How a mother who was too busy working and raising a family of five to give me any attention—had shaped my sense of self-worth. How my often-contentious relationship with my four sisters, had very much created an awareness, firstly that I was very different from women, but that I almost had to become feminine in order to feel accepted by them. I saw what my Catholic upbringing had taught me about guilt and shame and why I held so much of both.

Watching these visions, I felt I was a spectator of my life watching a movie screen of big events, feelings and conditioning. To have that eye-witness perspective helped me to be more objective about who I was—more discerning—the same way that a spectator at a sports game can often see the plays more clearly than the players down on the field.

The morning after ceremony, after saying goodbye to Pedro and arranging to see him again later that week, I walked into the misty Cusco Street outside the magical cattle shed, feeling as though I had been dancing all night at a cosmic party. I was exhausted but excited that I had just *survived* the most intense, bizarre, beautiful, and otherworldly experience of my life. I somehow made it home and crawled into bed beside Ursula and fell immediately into a deep sleep.

TINNITUS—A GIFT?

How can a loud ringing in one ear that never shuts off be a gift? Add the fact that with only one *good* ear, I lost the ability to use triangulation to pinpoint where a sound is coming from. If somebody says "Alan", unless I'm looking directly at them, they could be speaking to me from anywhere within a 360-range and I would have difficulty locating them.

The fact is that now in conversation, I have to give my absolutely undivided attention when someone is talking to me. I am completely focused. The level of attention I need in order to participate in conversations has given me the gift of developing an intensely high level of focus, so that I can devote 100% of my attention to my conversation partner.

This has been a huge asset for me as I am able to focus so attentively on my client in a healing session.

Afternote:

After seventeen years of drinking Ayahuasca, I recently went to a retreat in Peru, led by a Huni Kuin Pajé Shaman, Bire. I was told very clearly by the medicine that this retreat was about healing my hearing and I was to focus deeply on this process. Following the retreat, I am happy to report that the hearing in my Tinnitus-affected ear (my left ear) has improved by about fifty percent.

MEETING GOD

A single glance of Heaven,
Is enough to confirm its existence.
~ ABRAHAM MASLOW

Acouple of days later I had convinced Ursula and another friend to attend a ceremony. There were just the three of us *gringos* (Westerners). This was a good payday for Pedro, since he charged us way more than he did the Peruvian locals, because we had the resources to pay more. We were happy to pay *gringo rates* to help support him.

After the preliminaries, we drank the interesting-tasting brew, and it was lights off.

Even before Pedro starting singing, I went straight into a powerful vision of Death. It was clear that it wasn't my own death, nor did I have the feeling that I had died. It was simply that I was experiencing what it was like to be dead. Simply put, I was spirit. No element of my human experience remained other than my awareness, my imagination and my ability to discern what I was experiencing.

Is that all that we carry as part of our spirit nature? Is that pure consciousness?

Death is Divine. More accurately, it's the states beyond life that I name here as death. The expiration of life does not end it all: that is far from the truth of what I was being shown. Life is so simple without a human form, when you don't have senses or feelings to react to. My ego, which is just a reflection of my thoughts, was dissolved, allowing me to move beyond the container of viewing myself.

Expansiveness, vastness, lightness, blissfulness and freedom from negative emotions and reactions. I was with my spirit self, but I was not alone. There is no aloneness as spirit, as we are one with creative Source, as much as we are with our spiritual individuality. My spirit in Alan's body is my own, unique spirit and yet all spirit is oneness with everything in existence. I was a part of the matrix of creation and yet I had my own individual journey within it. I was the one experiencing my spirit essence, in the same way I experience the human paradigm.

To be fully present at each moment is a natural spiritual state that requires no additional focus or energy.

Just floating free

To be me in my Divinity

I was pure vibration—white light.

If this is our natural state, then why would we desire a human life to take us away from it? We experience separation from spirit and we struggle to bring ourselves back to it. That is the dilemma also known as the Cosmic Joke. Our natural state is the state of bliss and all-knowing and yet as humans, we spend our lives generally separate from these states, and then we put so much energy getting back to what is always there in our hearts. It is the ego that takes us away from connecting to our spirit, our Christ consciousness, Buddha Nature, Emptiness—Our Divine State.

But why does spirit even choose to enter the human form? Why bring that on himself/herself/itself when you have to leave such a beautiful, blissful reality? Is it to evolve? Without human senses or ego, spirit could not evolve in the same way or maybe at least, not as quickly. It is our natural state to continue to evolve within our own spiritual essence. How would spirit evolve just floating in space? It is within the challenges of being in embodied form that allows an advancement of soul learning.

God continues to evolve. God is all life and life in itself perpetuates the evolutionary journey. Even the trees, the plants, the animals, the clouds, the stars, the sun, the water, the mountains—they also face challenges in their universal process of survival. It is always within the challenges that growth comes. When you come back to pure consciousness, you connect with yourself in your truth. It's getting back there that is the sublime process of growth, which is also very often the challenge.

These realizations and many others flooded through me. It could have been in a second, or it could have taken hours. This was all before Pedro started singing his first *Icaros*! I had my journey even before the journey began! Pedro's singing pulled me back into my body. I was at peace. To recognize that my human self was simply a vessel of evolution allowed me to have peace with myself: my physicalness.

What I was seeing aligned with and expanded on my own belief systems around the afterlife. I was given more clarity. If I didn't believe in reincarnation and spirits, I'm not sure I would have had the same experience. It was not completely new information I was being given, just more awareness around that belief. More depth of understanding.

Ursula was on a mattress next to me. This was her first psychedelic experience—ever. I checked in with her to see if she was ok. "Oh yes fine, nothing's happened yet!"

70

It was in that response that I had my first realization that everyone's experience on the Ayahuasca journey is a different one. Even with the same medicine, the same songs, the same energy, the same night.

My life has never been the same since. Amongst other things, I have no fear of my own mortality—the cause of so many other human conditions. I feel my experience was similar to a near-death experience that often has the benefit of changing one's understanding of life.

AN UNEXPECTED TURN
OF EVENTS

We may turn to God,
When our foundations are shaking.
Only to find out
It is God who is shaking them.

~ HEBREW PROVERB

The experience I had during my second Ayahuasca ceremony helped me tremendously when I returned to my hospice work in California. I could sit by the bedside of dying patients knowing in my heart, that the client was going to a place of peace and expansion: a happy place! At the bedside, I would sometimes act as a bridge between this physical, three-dimensional world and the spiritual world on behalf of my client. This is the shamanic service of a *Psycho Pomp*. It could be seen as spiritual handholding as the dying person moves out of the physical plane. With my insights more developed now, I became a more effective psycho pomp and I feel I have helped many souls make their transition back home.

I had learnt this process in my trainings with Michael Harner, the grandfather of the renaissance of modern shamanism. Fortunately for me, he lived in Marin County, just across the Golden Gate Bridge from San Francisco where I lived.

Once I returned to San Francisco after Peru, I started to have more frequent interactions with my spirit guide Amantane. I had a lot of confidence in our connection ever since that morning when He helped to save my life. Since the ceremonies, I felt I understood Him better, as well as, His role in my life in the process of direct revelation.

One additional gift the ceremonies had given me was that for the first time, I was able to see Amantane, whereas up to that point I could only hear Him. He revealed himself to me as a South American Indian with a feathered crown. He looked like he was in his mid 60's, though I knew he was timeless. He was bare chested and only wore a leather loin cloth. I felt grateful to be able to look into his dark eyes for the first time.

I met him at the end of a mountain path, where he beckoned me to follow him up the winding path, that eventually led to a cave in the mountain side. Inside the cave was a circle of male elders standing around a fire. Amantane proceeded to join the circle and he then introduced the Council of Elders. I was guided to go to each one individually and look each one in the eyes with deep respect. They invited me to dance around the fire with them and deepen our connection. I was told that they would be there whenever I needed additional help with healing or with receiving guidance.

From this point on, Amantane often took me to the council to receive teachings and advice, always meeting me in the same place on the mountain path. This has been less frequent in recent years.

Whilst sitting at the bedside of the dying shortly after my return from Peru, something else became clearer that forever changed the direction of my life.

A PATIENT HAD JUST DIED

I had just returned home to San Francisco, California after spending six months living in Cusco, Peru. I was still absorbing the ceremonies I experienced with Maestro Pedro and trying to understand their meanings. The experiences themselves had been incredibly strong and mind expanding, but they hadn't healed my tinnitus, though I reveled in the beauty and power of what I had witnessed. I knew I was different now, but I couldn't quantify how exactly I had changed.

It was my first night back at my hospice shift. A man in his mid-seventies, had just died. Sitting at his bedside, I witnessed him take his last breath. Then it was peace; no more suffering; no more struggles with duality. I started meditating and praying for the peaceful journey of his soul.

As I sat there with my eyes slightly open, I saw light grey smoke leaving his body, wafting up from his nostrils, his ears and his mouth towards the ceiling of the hospice ward and then disappearing.

Is this his spirit or life force leaving his physical body? I asked myself.

I had never seen this before and I wondered if I was making it up. Because of my shamanic training, I understood that we make everything up anyway, so what did it matter? If it seemed real to me, then it was real.

In that moment, I said to myself—*Something's different, isn't it?*

Amantane responded, **"Yes, it is—YOU ARE A HEALER. THIS IS YOUR PATH FOR THE REST OF YOUR LIFE!"**

The words were clear and hit me like a thunderbolt.

Of course, that's right! I AM a healer. I responded with clarity and confidence.

A flash of insight hit me. *It all makes sense now! The path of my life has been an apprenticeship. I have been learning so many great tools that I can use to help others. Why have I been on these internal and external journeys? Why have I volunteered in hospice for so long? It has all been a training!*

I knew instinctively that Amantane would not have uttered the words, *"You are a healer,"* until I was ready to say *YES* when I heard them. The Ayahuasca ceremonies had given me the alignment I needed for the last little nudge. Amantane's timing and phrasing, as always, was impeccable.

Finally, all the experiences of my life, the challenges, the depression, the travels, developing self-awareness, the conditioning, the expansion of critical thinking—everything was crystallized into a moment of realization: nothing I had experienced in my life was futile or a waste of time. Everything had led me here to this point, to this moment, where suddenly I knew my life's purpose.

From that precise moment sitting at the bedside of a dead stranger on that Thursday evening in San Francisco in early 2006, I have not wavered from that knowledge—that calling— that truth. For that is who I am, have always been and always will be—a Healer.

I AM A HEALER

I came home from that hospice shift a different man. I knew that the trajectory of my life was going in a new direction in a way I had never dreamed. When Amantane uttered those prophetic words to me earlier in the evening: *"You are a Healer, this is your path for the rest of your life,"* I internally said YES. Then said out loud with equal conviction: *OF COURSE!*

I recognized that I was already doing healing work at the bedside of the dying. After all, I had been doing hospice volunteering for twelve years; week after week, month after month, year after year. Why had I been called to do this work with such commitment? I wanted to offer compassion and nurturing care to people who were suffering more than I was. The precise words *you are* meant I was already a healer and from that moment, without knowing how, I started healing people with clear intention and above all, with great confidence.

That evening I told Ursula what had happened. She said "You probably better go back to Peru!" That in itself was remarkable. Little did we know how much her suggestion was going to move our lives in completely different directions. We separated in 2012.

MY CAREER

My career path at this point was as a custom furniture maker. I was making high end, contemporary furniture for a broad range of clients all over the US. It was a great way to make a living: to be an artist, a craftsman making beautiful, museum quality pieces, for clients all over the country and occasionally overseas.

So, now what? What did it mean for me to be a healer? How was I going to fit that into an already busy life? How fully would I commit to this new path? These were questions that went through my head, but I knew instinctively that I would have to commit a 100% to this new career and life change.

A couple of months later, I was on an Ayahuasca retreat in a small retreat center called SpiritQuest Sanctuary outside of

Iquitos, Peru. This time I planned to immerse myself in the Sacred Medicine but, with the additional focus of learning about spiritual healing.

I was there to devote myself to the medicine ways, to understand how I could open up the channels of healing to help others change their lives. In my last ceremony with Maestro Pedro, he said to me: "I brought a part of your spirit back. Your life will be very different from now on."

I heard the words but couldn't fully absorb them. I didn't know what they really meant. Big life changes can really only be actualized over a period of time. With the advantage of time, you can see how changes have been significant, with the spaciousness from the beginning of the change, to the present moment, where change cannot be denied. I often tell my clients to give it six months before they see the full benefits of a session with me. At this point I knew something was different, I knew I was a healer but it would take time to see what Amantane had meant by—for the rest of your life!

Previously, I had a somewhat whimsical work life, trying my hand at new things. I never saw my general contracting, carpentry, furniture making, antique selling, house painting, importing crafts from Asia—or anything else I had tried—as a lifelong career. I felt I had a fearlessness at following through with choices I made, as I already had a track record of making big changes in my life.

I wasn't afraid to try something new but this complete change of direction wasn't just about career change, this was about a new Life Path. I was here on this retreat in Peru, not just for the experience, but to develop wisdom, awareness and skills for my healing path. I was here officially on an apprenticeship!

11

AYAHUASCA GRAND MASTER

All know the way,
But few actually walk it.

~ BODHIDHARMA

I had a pivotal teaching many years ago with a maestro of maestros, don Ignacio Diuri, who lived in the Peruvian Jungle town of *Infierno*. Infierno (Hell) was aptly named by the Spanish. A hot and humid town next to the Madre de Dios River, it has the worst mosquito and bug biting problem I've ever experienced. There is also a small insect called *pique* that bores into the skin under your toenails and lays eggs. If not extracted, these little buggers keep growing until the puss infected nest in your toes grow into a painful boil, with the baby piques growing under the skin and feeding off your blood. Yuck! Unfortunately, I found out about these little critters the hard way!

I went down to visit the maestro under the suggestion of my stateside teacher and mentor—Kamasqa Curandero, don Oscar Miro Quesada. Don Oscar had been friends with don Ignacio for years and he obviously had a deep reverence both for don Ignacio and for his work.

When I arrived and told don Ignacio why I had come, and that don Oscar had suggested I stay with him, he pointed to a very basic wooden hut on stilts and said "That's yours." Inside was an old mattress, a ripped mosquito net and some candles. Off grid living. Home for a month!

The first ceremony I had with don Ignacio in his rudimentary *Maloka* (round ceremonial building) was just the two of us. It started off very quietly. I wasn't really noticing much from the Medicine. I wasn't sure if don Ignacio was even awake, as he was making no sounds or singing any of the traditional Icaros (medicine songs that tend to stimulate the visionary quality of the sacred brew). Not a peep! I was a bit confused: this was new to me.

Previously, the ceremonies I had experienced with the Mestizo and Shipibo ceremonialists were filled with powerful songs that shape-shifted the whole experience, which can lead or influence the flow of energy and visions. Occasionally I would see the glow of don Ignacio's pipe, which preceded a puff of nebulous smoke into the air in my direction.

Ok I thought, this guy works differently. He has the highest recommendation from someone whose opinion I regard highly and trust implicitly. This man must be working like a Zen Master and doing so very quietly in the subtle realms. I have to start paying attention to what he is doing, rather than what is happening to me. So, I focused on him. I tried to connect into his energy field. What is he trying to teach me? How is he working in his unique way?

At some point around midnight, I said: *It's okay don Ignacio, you go to bed. I'm OK. I will just stay here alone.* After some back and forth, he shuffled off outside the Maloka. That was when the *shit hit the fan!* Immediately, the swirling and swooping energy of the medicine that I was more accustomed to, started to ignite feelings of fear and confusion inside of me and I became disoriented, not remembering where I was. I crawled outside and purged the purge of the Damned. I couldn't stop. I didn't know where my hut was and I couldn't move to get there even if I wanted to.

After a timeless journey into the depths of my insecurities and fears, all the while vomiting like I couldn't turn off the purge tap (and I'm not a quiet vomiter), I heard a rustling in don Ignacio's makeshift hut. A few minutes later, he was standing in front of me with a lit Mapacho. He blew smoke into my crown with three puffs. "You'll be OK now," he said. Immediately I stood up, walked to my hut, got into bed and went straight to sleep. *You little Pixie*, I thought to myself as I moved into semi-consciousness.

What I experienced with don Ignacio was true mastery. I recognized that not only was he working differently than the other Ayahuasqueros I had worked with—he was working softly and gently.

Prior to this experience, I had always thought that these ceremonies were meant to be turbulent and dramatic. The more extreme the experience, the more highly I regarded the maestro. I realized that don Ignacio had nothing to prove. He had transcended his ego and any macho desire to look good or impress anyone. This was vastly different from a lot of the other ceremonial experiences I'd had. Of course, I hadn't realized this till now.

Ceremonies just didn't have to be that hard. Ayahuasca didn't have to kick your butt to make a point or to evoke transformation.

LIFE DOESN'T HAVE TO BE THAT HARD

I realized that the ceremony of don Ignacio was a metaphor for the way I wanted to live my life. The *mantra* came to me: *Life doesn't have to be that hard!* If it was hard, I was the one making it so. All my inner resistance and tension caused me to struggle. If I could just get to that place of simplicity inside myself that was free of resistance, I could live a happier, healthier and more fulfilled life.

From that point on, Grandmother has been a lot gentler with me: I guess She feels that I got the point!

True emotional and spiritual maturity is about being able to do things at the highest level, within my own parameters of awareness and to continually strive to become more aware from a place of humility and grace—as demonstrated by don Ignacio.

My time with that beautiful, gentle, deep man and the simple way he lived his life, fully devoted to the medicine path in his challenging village, has completely reframed my life and my healing path.

I hold deep appreciation to the now deceased maestro who seemed to embody that mantra with everything he did. Whether it was working in his field growing yucca, sharpening his machete, or listening to an overly loud transistor radio on his basic wooden patio—he did so with such a gentle focus and sweet nature of being. I am forever grateful for his kind teachings of humility and simplicity.

12

REWIRING THE BRAIN

My brain is only a receiver.
In the Universe there is a core
From which we obtain
Knowledge, strength and inspiration.
I have not penetrated into the secrets of this core,
But I know that it exists.

~ NIKOLA TESLA

I lead annual tours to South America to have my clients experience Peruvian indigenous healers and their medicine ways.
One of the tours I lead includes visiting sacred sites of the
pre-Columbian cultures of the Andean areas, primarily known
as Incan Sacred Sites.

The most famous of these restored ruins in the Sacred Valley
of Peru is Macchu Picchu, which is also the most visited tourist attraction in all of South America. I tend to focus on other
sites that hold a similar spiritual significance in the Sacred Valley such as Pisac and Ollantaytambo. These also transport the
visitor back into the rich history of cultures that left us carved
monolithic stones of granite which were often brought from
valleys far from their current locations. These stones have been

mysteriously hewn with exactitude and precision, interlocking with each other like a three-dimensional jig saw puzzle, and are usually accredited to the Incan Empire.

The four-ton rocks in the Temple of the Sun located in the powerful fortress known as Ollantaytambo (place to see down) is located at the confluence of three valleys. The sacred site is quietly observed by a massive rock formation in a mountain adjoining the site, representing an upturned face of Wiracocha: The Creator God. The level of craftsmanship required, is mind boggling.

I also lead groups to the Amazon Rainforest, to experience Ayahuasca plant medicine traditions primarily with members of the Shipibo tribe. They are renowned for their expertise in Ayahuasca healings and have been deeply steeped in those medicine ways for thousands of years. I generally take groups to Pucallpa, Peru, which is the primary city of Shipibo culture.

Several years ago, the ceremonies on my upcoming retreat were going to be guided by a Shipibo husband and wife team, both in their early eighties—Benjamin and Antonia Maui. I was really excited that they had agreed to lead our group in the retreat center, La Casa de La Madre. The center was owned and run by my good friend Cielo Tierra. She was an Australian woman who had been in this area known as Yarinacocha for more than fifteen years. Sadly, she died this week—at the time of writing. Cielo and I had been co-creating group retreats for several years in Pucallpa. I also participated in many personal retreats at her place over the years, with different maestros.

Benjamin had taught many students and had trained many esteemed Ayahuasqueros, spanning a long and arduous career. He is a well-known and highly regarded Shaman and had spent many years of his life living in remote jungle huts, training and doing traditional diets. He once told me that in his 80 years, he had probably spent a quarter of his life in a restrictive solitary dietary practice which enhanced his spiritual and healing gifts. This is a traditional way to apprentice with plants. Despite that time in solitude, he had managed to have eight children with Antonia and they have remained married for over six decades.

In typical Shipibo style in Ayahuasca ceremonies, Benjamin being the male, was the energetic driving force, with his rhythmic and powerfully sung Icaros. Antonia, being the female, did the energetic sweeping up and offered the nurturing softness that helps to keep you feeling safe in your body and to trust in the work. This is commonly the way in Shipibo ceremonies—a dance of the masculine and the feminine, using the power of opposites known as *Yanantin*. They had a very beautifully choreographed energy, as you can imagine, after six decades of leading ceremonies together.

Their work with us went very deep and there was a significant amount of purging within the group during our ten-day retreat. Cielo and I were their assistants, making sure the participants physical needs were taken care of—emptying buckets and wiping butts, if necessary. Always a fun job!

In general, the experience with the medicine is directly related to the intention of the ceremony leaders and the style and energy in which they sing and facilitate it. Setting a pure intention for healing is critical for the leaders and the participants in ceremony. Direct communication with the spirits of Ayahuasca and with the ceremonial space, has a very profound influence on the healing potential for all participants. Benjamin and Antonia were masterful in holding space, which allowed all the participants to take deep dives into their inner worlds.

One ceremony night, as the group was getting quieter following an intense earlier phase of the ceremony, I laid back to luxuriate in the stillness and peace. I was lying on my mat in the darkness enjoying the sounds of the cicadas, frogs and bamboo rats who were adding their vibrations to the jungle heartbeat that pulsed through the ceremonial Maloka. Antonia was singing in the high-pitched raspy way that the Shipibo women typically sing their haunting medicine songs.

All of a sudden, I felt a strange tingling sensation in my head. It was extremely unusual and a bit freaky; it felt as though someone was literally cleaning my brain. I sat up and saw Benjamin looking at me through the darkness and blowing smoke directly at me from his Mapacho cigarette.

He was looking intently towards me, unblinking. I was aware of the single mindedness of his focus. Incredibly, I felt like my brain was being recalibrated, as though a Rubik's cube in my head was clicking and rotating to create a reorganization of anything that was out of balance. I sensed that Benjamin was helping me step up my game and my capacity as a healer. He knew the path that I was on and that I was here to be of service to the people on retreat and also back home in the U.S.

It felt like he was doing what was necessary to give me a neurological and energetic upgrade and a re-alignment of my brain's neural pathways. I focused deeply and expanded my awareness as best I could, so I could try to learn how this gifted maestro worked in such an advanced way. This was new to me: I had never experienced this unusual brain activity before, in or out of ceremony. I knew that I was being given not just a healing, but a teaching at the highest level—for which I felt incredibly grateful.

This all lasted about ten minutes and then it was over. Benjamin turned and started to work on the person to my right. I laid down again on my mat in the darkness and surrendered to the healing moving through me. I now believe that this recalibration by Benjamin has allowed me to explore to a new depth, the art of working in the *subtle realms*.

With spiritual healing work of any type, the healer can only help a person to the level of spiritual and conscious awareness that the healer themself possesses. This session with Benjamin helped to deepen my awareness, which in turn supported me in helping my clients to a greater depth. Working in these subtle realms is done through focus, intention, skill and aligning within the energetic flow and *The Sweet Spot* of healing. One does not need to drink Ayahuasca to receive deep healing, however, learning how to do this work would have been very difficult for me without my Ayahuasca experiences.

In observing Benjamin working on me, I was amazed that these things were even possible. As I have mentioned before, observation of the maestros is how one learns in this tradition. I learnt a great lesson that night that has served me and subsequently my clients, in the years following that experience.

Now, let's explore some of the ways that Ayahuasca ceremonies may unfold for you and how to gain the most from these experiences.

CEREMONY

And those who were seen dancing
Were thought to be insane,
By those who could not hear the music.
~ FRIEDRICH NIETZSCHE

Ayahuasca potentiates your energy field, allowing it to become more expanded and open. You can also become more sensitive to the energy of the other participants and of the ceremonial space. As such, it's vital to have an energetically clean ceremonial space, even if it's a bedroom in an apartment in Los Angeles. It's important to create sacred space and treat it as such, with reverence and humility. This is the responsibility of the ceremony facilitator, who often, if trained well, will offer an *arcana* (fortress in *Quechua*), or a cleansing and protection song to protect the space and each individual participant.

In creating sacred relationship with guiding spirits such as Ayahuasca, it is also important to first ask permission to proceed with the ceremony in order to do the high-level spiritual work that consequently unfolds. I have found that if this is not done, often the *mareacion* (visions) can get blocked. Usually offerings of tobacco, tobacco smoke, coca leaves, water, prayer, food, etc., are ritually offered in gratitude as a *prepago* or pre-payment to the spirit world.

Following the energetic cleanse of the space and an introduction to the ceremonial process, there is often a pre-amble of what to expect from the ceremony, including the logistics, the cautions and an explanation of what you might experience in ceremony. This is particularly the case in the first ceremony—especially in Western run circles, but is very often not part of indigenous ceremonies in tribal villages. Each facilitator has their own unique way of offering the first ceremony introduction.

Prior to drinking, there is usually an opportunity to speak out loud your intention for the ceremony; most ceremonies are held at night and participants typically remain in silence once ceremony begins. Shipibo and many others hold ceremonies either completely in the dark or with low candle lighting.

I exclude the Brazilian traditions in this description, which typically are more community oriented with group singing and praying. Some Ayahuasca churches such as Santo Daime, have Christian rituals and prayers that involve all participants.

After drinking the Ayahuasca, you will possibly experience different levels of energetic, hallucinogenic, mystical and entheogenic (*experiencing God within*) activity. The first part is usually the most intense, which often comes on around thirty to forty-five minutes after drinking. This is where the DMT can activate your pineal gland most powerfully and the visions may start to take you into otherworldly experiences. This can seem as though you are being shown alternate realities, metaphysical or mind-expanding psychological aspects of who you are at a core level. You may also connect with fantastical beings or with the source of creation in this transcendent space. For the new participant, it can often feel very intimidating, as you do not have any previous experience in maneuvering through the intensity. Sometimes the visions or the sacred geometry are so complex that it's difficult to effectively process the information.

The next phase, as you exit the peak experience, tends to soften and plateau and by now you will have developed a deeper sense of how the medicine is scanning and working with you. You can become more at peace with yourself. Your intention for the ceremony can become more refined, or you become more aware of how the medicine is directing energy to help resolve some of your core issues. You may also become more aware of what other participants are going through.

Often in first ceremonies the experience can be so otherworldly that you may be paying too much attention to what is going on in the room, than what is going on in yourself and the peak experience may be delayed as a result—if it even happens at all. By the second ceremony you will no longer be an Ayahuasca virgin and the tendency to be voyeuristic will lessen, allowing you to go deeper. Sometimes, you may just go straight for gold in the first ceremony and *break open*.

HAVE NO EXPECTATIONS

There are many internet videos, blogs and podcasts where people tend to recount their most momentous experience in ceremony. Many experiences, at least on the surface, don't make for interesting stories that are noteworthy enough to share on a podcast or a YouTube video. If you have previously watched or listened to some of these *momentous* accounts, you may develop unrealistic expectations of what the Ayahuasca experience should look like.

You will receive what you are ready for and what you are willing to allow.

THE INTENTION AND BREATH

Intention setting helps you to focus on a desired outcome and it helps to keep the initial focus narrow. Breathing in with long slow breaths at times during the ceremony, whilst repeating your intention, can help to take the medicine's vibratory resonance deeper into your energy field and in so doing, anchor the medicine deeper into your subconscious. Long slow breaths also help to calm and relax you during challenging episodes. This is a good reminder of how your breath can be a powerful ally during challenging times outside of ceremony. I have also found that repeating your intention during these times, can help to calm and center you. This is a good reason to keep your intentions short and specific.

A general focus of *I just want to live a richer, fuller life* is not as clear as focusing on what you feel is preventing you from living the richer, fuller life and also what would living a richer, fuller life look like.

If you are unsure of what you want, start by asking Grandmother to show you what could benefit you the most. Last but not least, always state your intention with deep humility and gratitude.

In a recent ceremony where I was a participant, after drinking a second glass, I felt the surge of Ayahuasca rushing through me like a tidal wave. I realized I wanted a new intention to the one I came into ceremony with, which I felt had been dealt with by the first glass. So quickly and just in the nick of time I said: *I want to be a better man.* The powerful embrace of the medicine quickly took me over and She spoke:

"Alan, first let me help you to refine your intention. How about, Grandmother, help me to be the best man I can be. 'A better man' doesn't really give you my full benefits. Why not use my power to take you further and broader than your original intention called for?"

Of course, I immediately saw the sense of this. Afterwards, I could feel the fingertips of spirit doctors pulling at my skin on my left hip, carefully removing energetic entanglements with women in my life, starting with the five women that I had grown up with in our little house in South London. I understood that this cleanse was about my *woman-wound* that had caused me to not fully trust women, and therefore not fully trust myself in relationships with them.

THE AYAHUASCA DIET

The diet, or dieta, is in itself an intention setting. Your willingness to follow a strict diet is a nod to your commitment to your well-being. It is more than a specific diet; it is a promise, an investment to your higher self. There is a general overview of what an Ayahuasca preparation diet should and should not include, which varies from tribe to tribe and facilitator to facilitator. *Dieta* includes anything you put into your body. In addition to specific foods and beverages, refrain from negative thoughts, aggressive music and film, or anything of a low density. Abstaining from these things is considered a form of physical and mental purification.

The diet is done to get you into alignment with the spirit world. The food part of the diet tends to be bland and does not stimulate your senses in the same way as food cooked in oils with salt and spices. Abstaining from sex and orgasms can also be seen as aligning yourself more with the spirit world. Spirit does not have human senses and does not get stimulated by taste, touch, smells or the sexual act and does not experience physical pleasures. The diet also makes your health conditions more transparent to the plant spirits.

Paying it forward to the spirit world through the dieta is equivalent to you saying: *I am willing to commit to my well-being by aligning with the spirit world as best I can.* That clear intention to the spirit of Ayahuasca and any other spirit energies that are present, provides the ideal landscape for what follows, both during and after the ceremony.

The healing begins as soon as you sign up for ceremony. Use this time well in treating your body with kindness and respect. You will notice how your mind craves that which it is restricted from having. I have done many three to four day fasting vision-quests during which I consumed only water. I used this time to watch my mind working with hunger and always noticed it as a mind craving, more than a body need.

EVERYTHING IS RELEVANT

These are the times in life
When nothing happens—
But in the quietness
The soul expands.
~ ROCKWELL KENT

Some participants may report that "Not much happened!" This is not uncommon, especially in the first couple of ceremonies. Everyone's experience is different of course, but it's possible that *something did happen* but, that it was more subtle than the person was expecting. It's possible that the medicine was *scanning* the participant and preparing them for future ceremonies. Sometimes someone might need a couple of ceremonies under their belt to feel safe before they surrender to more powerful experiences, as they learn to trust the facilitator, the space, and the non-ordinary nature of the work.

The times you feel that nothing is happening are the times to listen to yourself: sit with the feeling that nothing is happening. Is it your resistance within *nothing is happening*? You can be sure that something is happening but what are you looking for within this happening? How are you listening or paying attention? How well did you prepare for this experience?

You might pay attention to the degree that your ego is trying to control events, and notice that the attachment to your beliefs may be so strong, that you cannot fully benefit from the expansive potential of this healing opportunity. You are resisting the experience. This is in itself a great teaching and if you are open enough, it can allow you to look at how you resist life.

Over the years I have witnessed many people (myself included), put the blame for not having a strong experience on the facilitator, the medicine, the other participants, or on anything other than themselves. Some people feel safer to remain in a state of denial, rather than enter the expansive world of being fully awake.

It takes commitment to benefit fully from these experiences. If you have come to the ceremony simply to have an *ayahuasca experience*, you will not benefit as much as if you engage in this moment as a fully transformational opportunity.

There is no direct correlation between the perceived depth of your experience and the actual depth of healing that you receive.

The amount and quality of any visuals you receive can vary greatly. You may be shown symbols or metaphors, allowing you to tap into a hidden memory held in the cells of your body, where true healing lies. Even if you don't experience many visuals, you will still benefit from the plant's wisdom. Everyone is different and has a different healing path.

RELEASING AND PURGING

In Ayahuasca ceremonies, the main way to release energy blocks is through purging. This can be in the form of vomiting, diarrhea, tears, yawning, sweating, etc. Sounds attractive right? It can be hard work on the body and mind and can be psychologically very challenging, as a lot of inner fears can rise to the surface preceding the purge.

The purging releases toxins from the physical, mental, emotional and spiritual bodies, in many dimensions at the same time. It is unlikely that you will know exactly what you are purging and why. It's always a good idea to thank the medicine after a purge as you are receiving healing and cleansing on many levels. It's probably like nothing else you have ever experienced.

"I HAD A BAD CEREMONY"

I have heard many people describe their ceremony experience as bad. I feel it's important to reframe that description. There are not really *good* or *bad* ceremonies. There are just ceremonial experiences. That which may be described as bad may simply be unpleasant or even, very unpleasant. Maybe it's a moment where some painful or challenging emotions have come up; perhaps old beliefs, experiences, judgments, or resentments that Abuela has exposed?

The experiences that are often characterized as *bad* tend to be the most beneficial in the long term—more beneficial than feeling blissful all the time. The fact that we may fear something means that it is significant to us, and we are likely to gain the most insight by looking at it—thereby eventually overriding the fear around it. Through facing fear and other difficult emotions, we have an opportunity to explore the gold nuggets that they represent. Rather than seeing these experiences as bad, we can choose to see them as hard, challenging, or even juicy! Sometimes we need something to be hard, so these challenging experiences can help us appreciate those moments when things are easy and joyful.

People can have a psychotic episode as a result of drinking Ayahuasca, but this is usually because they came into the ceremony with a history of psychosis. The medicine can also contraindicate with certain pharmaceuticals causing neurological imbalances. It's important that nobody with a history of psychosis or mental illness drinks Ayahuasca, for their own safety and the safety of the other ceremony participants. If this is ignored, the outcome could indeed be bad.

WAYS THAT WE DISTRACT OURSELVES

The mind is tricky and without realizing it we can develop strategies to distract ourselves in ceremony. The best way to *be* in ceremony is to sit up straight, breathe with a relaxed breath and stay focused, with minimal movement—except when purging or going to the bathroom. You are likely to gain the most from this strategy.

Some ways that you can be avoidant are to:

- fidget or move around—as in flailing arms and legs
- make unnecessary noises, including talking or loud sobbing
- continually open and close your eyes
- focus on others rather than on yourself
- get annoyed with others
- decide you want to be one of the ceremony healers
- seek an inordinate amount of attention from the facilitators

It is of course okay to lie down and many retreat centers provide sleeping pads rather than chairs or back jacks. My personal preference is to sit up throughout the whole ceremony.

THINGS TO BRING

Some ceremonial spaces don't have much room for personal items but there is usually enough space for you to bring:

- A favorite crystal or protective talisman which you can place by your personal space or be invited to place on a central altar.
- A closable water container.
- A refreshing spray or uplifting essential oil such as Palo Santo.
- A feather fan to cleanse stuck energy off your body or to simply fan yourself.
- A face cloth (you will usually be provided with paper towels or toilet paper), to wipe your mouth or face after purging vomit or tears.
- A musical instrument to play, if you are invited to do so.

I have seen participants bring favorite cuddly toys to help them get into memories of their toddler selves or to help them feel safe.

OTHER PROTOCOLS

Talking in ceremony is generally taboo, as is interpersonal interactions, due to the fact that Ayahuasca works on each person according to their individual needs. Talking to another participant can distract them from this optimum healing experience, which is after all, why they are there—as are you.

Drinking water is not recommended after drinking the Ayahuasca, as you may purge due to the water rather than because of a toxin or energy block. It is okay to swill your mouth with water and spit into your bucket. At some point in the ceremony, you may be invited to drink water.

Leaving the ceremonial space during ceremony except to use the rest room is frowned upon, except if you are with a helper. To leave the ceremony without permission from the facilitator, who will most likely be aware that you have left, could be dangerous, especially if you have the intention of not coming back. You are also breaking the energy of the sacred circle created at the opening of ceremony, and your departure may affect this container.

The ceremony most often finishes with a closing ritual during which the energy can be released and the energy field of the participants can be sealed, allowing them to come back fully into their bodies. It's important that all participants are present at the closing of ceremony, to allow for a complete discharge of the energetic container that was built during the ceremony and for a closing of the ceremonial space.

*In the next chapter I share how you can gain
the most from your Ayahuasca experience
through post ceremony integration.*

INTEGRATION

Once you've tasted alignment
Nothing else will do.

~ ABRAHAM

Once the energy blocks have been removed through purging or extraction by the Shaman and the energetic causes of their associated restricted reactions have been released, the body can then naturally start to align itself to the homeostatic state of healing.

The mind however, often needs a bit more coaxing and takes a while to catch up to the body's shift. Because the subconscious responds best to repeated reinforcement of a belief or condition, it's important to repeatedly inform your subconscious of the changes that you want to occur. This is done through developing new and improved belief systems. In other words, it doesn't just do itself.

Many people who have sat in my ceremonies think that Ayahuasca is a magic pill to transformation. The truth is that Ayahuasca is, amongst other things, a clarifier and a roto rooter for clearing out the physical, mental and emotional energetic blocks. These blocks prevent people from connecting to their hearts and souls. Once the blocks are cleared, it takes time and commitment to integrate the new patterns. The subtle layers are by nature subtle, and one may not notice the changes until after they have happened. It's important to pay attention and support the potential shifts. This requires diligence and action.

HOW COMMITTED ARE YOU?

When I work with clients in the integration and spiritual coaching process, I ask them questions like the following:

1. What do you feel are the opportunities that have opened up for you?
2. What do you feel is possible and how do you see it working out?
3. Do you have an action plan?
4. How will you live from your heart and your higher states of being?
5. How will you honor the work you were willing to commit to in ceremony, to make changes in your life, to your dietary intake, your thought patterns, your delusions, your habits, your belief systems, your reactions and responses?
6. What are your passions and how will you follow them?

I ask them to ask themselves: *How committed am I to changing my life?* Grade that commitment level from 1–10, with 10 being the most committed. If they answer a number below 8, I ask, what is required to make it a 10?

It often takes a skilled human intermediary to ask the hard questions and to be the accountability partner for your follow through. That could be a professional coach, a therapist, or a friend you may have met at an Ayahuasca retreat. I recommend it be someone who has experience in psychedelic integration.

When I first drank Ayahuasca, I didn't know anyone else who had done so, and I didn't even know about integration following ceremony. Maestro Pedro said nothing to me about it, as it was not part of his cultural understanding. Fortunately, I was in my mid 40's and had been a practicing Buddhist for a decade and a half, so I had a certain degree of emotional and spiritual maturity. I also already had many experiences with psilocybin and LSD, that helped me navigate the psychedelic terrain, allowing for my re-entry into *normal reality* to be relatively painless.

Had I been ten or twenty years younger, I imagine it would have been more challenging, not having anyone to talk to about it. The one question I did clearly ask myself was—*Now What?* I knew something was different but I didn't have any guidance as to what to look for or expect.

When I was told "You're a healer. This is your path for the rest of your life," the *now what* was pretty clear and I took action and multiple ongoing actions since that time to support my path as a healer. I knew that some choices I had to make would be scary and daunting: such as getting divorced, selling my house and leaving my beloved San Francisco to eventually open a retreat sanctuary in Mt. Shasta. If I hadn't followed through with an *action plan*, the benefits would not have been as pronounced and transformative.

Ayahuasca can help you to deepen your self-awareness so you can understand your mind more clearly. She is also very effective at helping to heal physical conditions. But if you don't integrate the Ayahuasca healings by making informed decisions over how you treat your body, you will not benefit from the deepest and most transformative opportunities presented from the journey.

Recognize that after a time, everything becomes normalized. The euphoria that may follow ceremonies will stabilize and everything will reach an equilibrium, so that you don't notice that euphoric feeling in the same way. This doesn't mean that shifts aren't still happening: they are just moving deeper into the subconscious and may be operating vibrationally at a higher level. It's important to design practices to keep yourself at that higher level, such as eating high vibration foods, meditating, spending time with trees and clean water sources and thinking and talking positively. These lifestyle changes support your internal changes.

The Ayahuasca journey to healing is part of a process and not a single event, so it has to be seen as a process rather than a magic pill. This is why the integration period is so important. Individual Ayahuasca ceremonies can help to peel away layers of resistance, but this doesn't happen to the full extent in a weekend, that it may over an extended retreat or, with additional dieta practices.

The duration of post-ceremony integration can last 180 days or more. In that time, you may notice raised levels of empathy, so be gentle with yourself. For the most powerful transformation, I recommend developing an attitude of surrender and acceptance, rather than expectation. Healing may not take the form you were expecting. Honor what is, or what you may become—hopefully a better version of yourself.

LIFE DOESN'T HAPPEN TO YOU: IT HAPPENS BECAUSE OF YOU

Ayahuasca is definitely not the lazy person's way to healing and you will not create a permanent shift if you are not willing to support that shift through behavior and mindset changes. If your behaviors and habits are exactly the same after an Aya-huasca ceremony, you will not benefit from all the energy re-leases you receive through the purging and any extractions.

Why put yourself through the often-demanding Ayahuasca ceremonies if you aren't willing to change other aspects of your life? Just doing it because your friends are doing it, or to get an Ayahuasca badge of honor, is probably going to be a big waste of time and money. Remember, *actions have consequences.*

I have heard many times "Alan, the ceremony was amazing but now I feel pretty much the same as before," to which I re-spond—*Well what changes have YOU made to support the changes you were looking for?*

"Uh, not much really!" Enough said.

You must accept responsibility over your changes in life. After all, the patterns you don't like are happening because of you. You may feel that they are just happening to you: a run of bad luck, a bad relationship, or lack of abundance, but they are happening due to your daily choices and behaviors. In life—including in working with Ayahuasca—you have to be vigilant and keep your focus on the potential outcome you intend for yourself. Consistency is key.

Many times, you may say you want change, but you don't behave in a way that opens the way for the changes you claim to seek. If you want to have deeper relationships, you need to show up in a deep way to your relationships. If you want a healthier body, you need to show up for your body and change your diet and workout habits.

IT TAKES TIME

My clients often call me up six months after our healing session and tell me how much their lives have changed. The Ayahuasca healing experience unfolds over a lengthy period. Yes, you can receive messages and guidance during the ceremony itself that can point you in a new direction, or show you where you need to shift your mindset or habits. The real work starts when you commit to using that knowledge and wisdom to actually create the life you seek. That is the power of integration! The changes you make literally become integrated into your subconscious and energy body and your life manifests a permanent change in behavior, beliefs and wellbeing. To benefit as much as possible from the plant teacher, stay flexible, curious, and open-minded before, during, and after your ceremonies.

Look back in your life and remember how making decisive decisions has changed the course of your life. Use this time of integration to use all your mental and intuitive capacity, combined with the accentuated clarity from ceremony, to propel you forward with more confidence and power.

It's good to ask yourself open-ended questions following ceremony and a good way to integrate those is to keep a journal or Ayahuasca Workbook. You could name it something like *The Journal of Personal Liberation* and use it for self-inspiration, even putting in inspiring quotes from others.

Some good questions to pose to yourself are:

- What does my soul want me to know?
- What does happiness feel like?
- I make a commitment to my well-being by . . .
- What I am willing to admit is . . .
- How can I love myself more?
- The changes I am willing to make are . . .
- How do I feel about myself, right now?
- What is my life's purpose?
- The things I can do to stay in a high vibration are . . .

All the above apply to life whether or not you drink Ayahuasca. Ultimately *the bucks stops here* and you have to be willing to commit to whatever changes you wish to make, especially if you have had a lifelong impediment. The Ayahuasca experience could be seen as a milestone towards a dramatic shift. Don't waste the opportunity. Use the above suggestions to help you with any shift you have been unable or unwilling to change. Create your own suggestions based on your biggest needs.

SPINNING OUT

Sometimes in ceremony the incoming information is too big and vast for your brain to comprehend, and it simply shuts down to protect itself. This is known as spinning out. Participants may have periods of time during and after ceremony that appear blank. Some of this information may filter through over the coming months. It's often helpful to do daily periods of automatic writing for several weeks after the retreat has ended. This means putting your pen on a page of a journal or simple notebook and writing without thinking or stopping for 10 to 15 minutes, (I recommend 700-800 words). When you read it back, you may be surprised at what your subconscious mind has revealed.

DON'T BLAME THE VINE

Oftentimes following ceremony, I hear people making grand statements about how their life is going to change in some big way as a result of their powerful experience.

I hear things like: "Ayahuasca told me to . . . "

- Leave my wife.
- Leave my job.
- Tell my boss what a Dick he is.
- Give all my money away and go live in an ashram in India.
- Downsize and live in a Tiny House.
- Start eating meat.
- Become vegan.
- Start leading Ayahuasca ceremonies.
- Go back to school.

Of course, there is nothing wrong with making life changes following Ayahuasca retreats and in fact it's encouraged. It's usually best however, to give some spaciousness between the Ayahuasca experience and making some momentous life change, as it takes time for the medicine's effects to fully filter through. The crucial thing is to take full responsibility for making the decision yourself and not put the *blame* on Ayahuasca's shoulders.

In saying "Ayahuasca told me to . . . " you are giving responsibility over to another power and in so doing, you are giving your power away.

A few years ago, I had a big fall out with a close friend and I wasn't sure what to do about it so, I did a personal Ayahuasca session around the issue. I saw the clarity of the situation and was guided by Grandmother to end the relationship. A couple of days later I called up my friend and said tearfully: *This is hard for me but Ayahuasca told me I have to end the friendship.* On putting the phone down, I felt like such a loser for saying that. I didn't have the strength to take responsibility for my decision but gave the responsibility over to the medicine. In giving the power to Ayahuasca, I took power away from myself. I vowed to never do that again.

Being healthy, speaking honestly, being decisive, setting clear boundaries: they're all about holding personal responsibility and *not giving your power over to another force.*

I have never again said, *Ayahuasca told me to . . .* It's way more powerful and assertive to say, *I have decided to . . .* and in so doing, being fully responsible with your decision.

SPIRITUAL BYPASSING

I also hear many people say in the same way "Spirit told me to . . . " Of course, it's a great asset to be guided by spiritual wisdom and to pay attention, as I have continued to do since my original encounter with Amantane. Spirit guides us, as does universal consciousness, and often it's difficult to differentiate between the two and it doesn't really matter. As long as the guidance is benevolent and wise and you feel you have free will to decide or not, then follow through if it feels right. It's important to take full responsibility and not hand it over to Spirit—otherwise that is *spiritual bypassing.*

In the next chapter I put forward some ideas about how Ayahuasca heals based primarily on my own experiences, direct revelations and personal reflections.

HOW AYAHUASCA HEALS—
Some ideas

Our wounds are often the openings
Into the best and most beautiful parts of us.

~ DAVID RICHO

Full disclosure—nobody knows how Ayahuasca heals, any more than anyone knows how anyone heals—beyond theories. There is an innate body intelligence that kicks in when the right conditions and environment are provided to do what it knows very well how to do—*heal or get sick*. I cannot state definitively how Ayahuasca heals and I claim no empirical wisdom on the matter, nor have I done clinical studies to back up any of my suggestions.

In the same way, I can't honestly claim that I know how I help people heal, nor how much my contribution plays a part in their healing. I can assume that both Ayahuasca and I are doing something to help clients benefit long term. From within that great mystery, an alchemical change happens.

As this is not a book about scientific research on Ayahuasca, I suggest you do your own due diligence regarding scientific, peer-reviewed studies. By typing *how Ayahuasca heals* into a search engine, I found many wonderful articles and scientific studies. I also highly recommend Rachel Harris's excellent and well researched book *Listening to Ayahuasca*.

HIDDEN IN THE DEPTHS

Ayahuasca's ability to reveal deeply buried traumatic memories allows for the processing and healing of events surrounding those memories. This facilitates the release of energetic and psychological causes of the originating limiting conditions, which may have manifested as physical sickness of some type. This is one of Ayahuasca's greatest attributes.

Have you ever seen photos of some of the monstrous looking creatures that spend their whole lives completely in the dark, at the bottom of the deepest ocean, never to be revealed in the light of day? An internet search will show the horrific looking creatures such as Scale Worms, Anglerfish and the Common Fangtooth. And yet, the sea creatures that live in the light close to the surface are some of nature's most beautiful creations—with a myriad of unbelievable colors and designs—that are a joy to behold. This could be seen as a metaphor of what happens when you bring long-forgotten memories to surface into the light: what you see, by a natural evolutionary process of nature, changes from ugliness into unimaginable beauty.

FACING YOUR FEARS

Often, in Ayahuasca ceremonies, you will experience fear-based phenomena such as: being attacked by demons, gargoyles or other imaginary beings. Whether you see images or just feel fearful sensations in your body, the effects are the same. Facing your fears is one of the biggest opportunities Ayahuasca can give you. You may have been on the run from those fears or anesthetized yourself against them your whole life, (with drugs, food, sex, alcohol, etc.) and yet, in these precious moments in ceremony you are being given golden opportunities to enter the darkness to dispel them. You may blame people or experiences outside of yourself, but the truth is, the responsibility for these feelings lie inside of you.

Once you decide to face these fear-based images in ceremony, they can almost miraculously disappear. If the fearful encounter doesn't go away, then that is probably because you are still running from it. It's very simple:

You fully face it = it goes away. You don't fully face it = it remains.

FEAR OF SNAKES

From an early age I had a fear of snakes. It felt completely irrational to me, having grown up in South London where the only snakes I ever saw were harmless grass snakes. I can only assume it developed after watching an old Johnny Weissmuller Tarzan film I had seen on TV. Just the thought of them gave me the shivers!

One warm afternoon in 1986, I was lying in a hammock in the garden outside my cattle shed home in the village of Manasbal, Kashmir, when I started hearing birds squawking frantically. I looked over in their direction and saw a few Blue Jays attacking what I instantly recognized as a King Cobra—the largest venomous snake in the world; he was slithering on the ground. Its venom will kill an average sized human in 30–40 minutes. I immediately understood that the birds were trying to protect their eggs or chicks in their nests that were up in the rafters of my shed. I was fascinated by the whole scene and walked closer to take a better look at the cobra, until I was about fifteen feet away. As I reflected on what I was doing, whilst also having a healthy respect for this dangerous reptile, I realized I wasn't holding any fear.

Oh, I'm not afraid, I said to myself: *I'm not actually afraid of snakes!*

This was a unique experience for me, as this was the first time in my life that I was in the presence of a very dangerous snake in the wild. Up to that point, it was only my imagination that had planted the suggestion that I was afraid of snakes. In confronting a snake, I realized my fear was just made up. Since that moment, I have completely lost my fear of snakes and have since come across many, in my travels in the jungles of South America.

When before had I ever been given an opportunity like this? In a split second, I got the chance to release the energetic and psychological cause of something I had held in my body for decades. This was a transformative moment.

Similarly, by confronting other fears in Ayahuasca journeys, I have dominated them by the growing awareness that they were implanted in my subconscious from an often-unknown source. What was required was for me to inform my subconscious that I no longer needed to react to these fears in the same old way.

I have often imagined myself like valiant St. George fighting off the Dragon. The Dragon being a metaphor for my fears. Doing battle was one way I overcame them, or just standing up to them with a warrior spirit's strong character—I prevailed over them. Once I did that, they no longer had power over me.

I can vividly remember a particular ceremony during a retreat outside of Iquitos, Peru in 2007. This third ceremony of a series of six was and still is, the scariest night of my life. I was being bombarded with bird headed humans pecking at me relentlessly for what seemed like days. There was no escaping them and believe me, I tried. I was cold with fear. I got through it. I survived. But I felt like I had died and was reborn. I went into the next ceremony with renewed vigor (though admittedly nervous) and an attitude of *Bring It On!* When they appeared again that night, I remember thinking—*Fuck it! I'm going in.* And I stepped right into the center of those *evil creatures.* They disappeared and never came back again that retreat. The remainder of the ceremonies were much more peaceful after my *dark night of the soul.*

Those creatures come back every now and then but now when they show up, I just say: *Not you again. You're not still trying that shit!* and they slink away with their tails between their legs.

BOOT CAMP FOR YOUR SPIRIT

Imagine you have just gone through a gut wrenching, tortuous and agonizingly hard Ayahuasca session like the one I just described and you experienced an ego death, like I did. This is the point where your ego is shattered and you are broken open and where now you are given a chance to come back from this death to live in a new, exalted way—with a new elevated level of personal power.

I believe that when we are put into traumatic situations, such as being a soldier in a war, getting sexually abused, or living in an unsafe environment as a child, we are being subjected to the will and control of another. Someone, who in that moment has authority over us. We do not choose to be in these particular situations. We experience feelings of powerlessness—having no choice in these moments—that causes us to react so deeply to the trauma response contained in these situations.

I have found that Post-Traumatic Stress Disorder (PTSD) occurs largely because the sufferer was not sovereign in their decision to go into the metaphorical or literal battle. They didn't choose the situation that caused the trauma they endured and had little or no control over what happened.

In comparison, doing battle with your demons (related to a traumatic event) within an Ayahuasca experience—is 100% your individual choice. Ayahuasca allows you to connect with the sovereign directives from inside yourself and in so doing, allows you to take back the power that you lost. Thus, enabling you to strengthen your spirit. With your newly fortified spirit, you will quickly notice a change in your trauma response. You can't intellectualize or talk your way to change. Dominate or elevate yourself above limiting patterns. Meet them full on to manage them.

One of the greatest attributes that Ayahuasca has to offer you, is in the strengthening of your spirit. With a strong spirit, you can start:

- Setting clear boundaries with yourself and others
- Developing self-love
- Making empowered choices
- Facing your fears and acting from a place of courage
- Developing confidence
- Focusing on hope rather than hopelessness
- Building personal sovereignty
- Holding full accountability

I re-emphasize, *to dominate,* as stressed to me by my Peruvian teachers, is about building spiritual strength, developing personal power and a stronger character. It means not giving in to your limiting inner voices. This doesn't mean you white knuckle it through or ignore those voices, it means you elevate yourself beyond their influence.

When you learn to do this in ceremony, you are equipped to imitate this new behavior out of ceremony and soon will find, you do not get triggered in the same old way.

Coming home from these sometimes-challenging experiences, allows you to appreciate what you have, rather than what you don't.

Thanks to my Ayahuasca experiences, I have let go of many fear-based, neurotic beliefs such as: fear of heights, fear of public speaking, fear of teaching, fear of being the center of attention, fear of loving deeply, fear of claustrophobia and fear of writing this book.

TOUGH LOVE

Over the many years I have worked with Ayahuasca, I have experienced challenging times, humbling times, isolating and connecting times, and the purging and emotional swings associated with this sacred and powerful teacher. I have had extremely uncomfortable dark nights of the soul and also had the most beautiful and uplifting ceremonies imaginable. I have seen and been absorbed by my true spiritual nature and experienced a transcendent connection to my own divinity. I have been wrapped in Angels' wings—for hours.

What divinity is or feels like is for each individual to interpret in their own way. Even if you are agnostic, you may be shown a view of reality that changes your perceptions and leaves you changed—to make sense of what spirituality means.

Ayahuasca has been a beautiful teacher for me, with both tough love and gentle prodding. There have been countless times in solo ceremonies in which She has kicked my butt and admonished me with: **"Who the fuck do you think you are?"** She has brought me to my knees in a pool of tears and vomit many times, only to tell me to get my ass up and start doing my work. She repeated back to me: **"Necesitas dominar, Alan,"** echoing my human teachers' insistence.

So, I would get up off my ass, wipe my nose and go back to the ceremonial space on my own and continue with my solo ceremony, as though I had a room full of people needing my help and support. The importance of solo ceremonies, being a facilitator, is to continue to work on myself to build my spiritual and psychological strength. In so doing, I have learnt how to hold sacred space, stay in my power, and elevate my consciousness above and beyond the intensity of the visions. I have to be strong to be able to handle any situation that may arise in a group setting.

I continue to learn from these deeply humbling and sometimes humiliating times. I call them my *Bitch Slaps for the Soul* which strengthen my character and redefine my personality. It is my Spiritual Warrior training!

EGO DEATH

Ego is an aspect of the human experience. Without ego we would not be experiencing this human life. The Ego Death you experience in an Ayahuasca ceremony refers to the release of a diminished view of yourself, or fear-based beliefs. These beliefs control your thoughts, actions and behaviors, which restrict your connection to your truth. The *death of the Ego* allows you (at least temporarily) to be free from whatever causes you to live in a spiritually contracted manner.

You can see ceremonies as pattern breakers that bring into question the validity of your beliefs. In breaking through the ego nature of your belief structures, you can arrive at a place of selflessness, and in so doing, see the futility of how your ego states have caused you to feel separation from yourself and others.

AYAHUASCA SEES YOU

Sickness, whether it be physical or emotional, is a very lonely experience. Your pain is your pain, even if you have a friend or loved one holding your hand and empathizing with you; you are the only one who can know what it's truly like. It is this isolation within a painful experience that can often feel like the weight of the world is on your shoulders and can intensify your suffering.

In an Ayahuasca ceremony, your awareness of a painful experience can become more expanded and universal. In feeling a greater connection to yourself, you can feel more *seen* from inside. In truly feeling seen, the trauma of the pain that you've been carrying can diminish just within that connection. She can feel like a loving mother, mopping your brow and holding you in support. She can engage with you and offer deep compassion for your suffering, as you receive guidance and strength from within the spirit realm.

When you go to the doctor's office and a kindhearted doctor *sees* you and is compassionate with you—rather than acting dismissively, you naturally feel more hopeful and cared for. In the same way, Ayahuasca, with Her ability to see you from the inside, can feel like the kind doctor who sees into your pain and supports you from the deepest place of your being.

MIND OVER MATTER

Ayahuasca can increase the level of your suggestibility and cause you to be subject to the influence of another. That's why *it's important that the facilitator be a person of integrity so that you can trust the intention for the ceremony.* The Shaman is in a powerful position to use the enhanced mental and emotional pliability of the participants, as an opportunity to maximize healing within them.

In ceremony, the Shaman may wear special robes and use jewelry, feather crowns and face paint designs with natural dyes and colorings from plants. Part of the reason for this is that it sets the Shaman apart from the other participants and helps to make him or her appear more impressive. It gives him or her authority in a similar way to the white coat of a doctor or the stripes and ribbons of a general's uniform; it commands respect. Some indigenous traditions also incorporate a lot of theater, like the macho strutting and bravado of northern Peruvian Huachumeros, the head-dress and energetic drumming and dancing of Mongolian Shamans, and the hypnotic trance dancing of the African San Bushmen.

The perceived authority of the shaman can lead to feelings of safety and trust in his ability to heal. This suggestibility factor might be one reason behind spontaneous healing. There's a belief, that the set and setting of the ceremonial process and rituals of Ayahuasca, can trigger spontaneous healing due to the person's expectations and trust in the Ayahuasquero. If a person expects the process to bring about a healing, then that person's own bio-chemistry may be activated for healing to occur naturally. There is a direct relationship between how strongly a person expects to have results and whether or not results occur. The stronger the feeling is, the more likely a person will experience positive effects.

I am not intending to diminish the cultural and symbolic meaning, nor the interpretation of the costumes or rituals, which are all valid and important to the tribe and culture where they are practiced. It's good to be aware that they also have a psychological impact that can enhance healing.

Of course, it is multi-layered; everything is relevant and if the person is healed, then it's really not important how it happened. There is a fundamental belief in wisdom traditions such as Shamanism, which is: *If it works—use it. If it doesn't—don't bother!*

This is what separates shamanic healing from traditional allopathic healing. Past healing events do not govern the outcome of future healing events and therefore it's not necessary to know the science, or have data related to outcomes of a specific treatment, for healing to happen.

AYAHUASCA AND SPIRITUALITY

We are all stars wrapped in skin,
the light you seek
has always been within.
~ RUMI

Many people report profound mystical experiences during and after ceremony that could lead to changes in perception. These can generate experiences of ego dissolution and subsequent feelings of limitlessness and a transcendental connection to everything. These experiences have been closely linked to improved quality of life. The expansion of conscious awareness within a mystical experience can leave you with the feeling that there is much more to life and so much more to you than you had ever imagined.

In ceremony, you may sense the entheogenic nature of the sacred brew where you access the God within. You are introduced to an expanded awareness around the nature of reality and the spiritual dimension. This may be similar to near-death experiences (NDE's), where your spirit leaves the physical form on its way to the vastness of the numinous realms beyond physical existence—until called back into the body. Many people recount seeing themselves surrounded by light and light beings or, the creative Source of *All That Is*. As with an NDE experience, you may receive messages and guidance from a higher source that may cause you to examine your current life and the changes you wish to make.

The use of entheogens can help you connect with *reality* from the heart, which is where your truth resides. When you connect more deeply with your heart, your choices will shift and be informed by your more expanded nature. You can then operate from a place of more love, more joy and more happiness. The more you open your heart to yourself, the more you make decisions that support your well-being. You will make choices that are from a place of deep self-reverence, instead of just thinking and reacting.

Ayahuasca is not traditionally used for seeking enlightenment or ending the cycle of human existence, as seen in many Eastern spiritual traditions. Traditional Shamanism is about being more fully you—integrated and whole, with both feet planted firmly on the ground and at the same time, being an interface with all of nature's spirituality and conscious aliveness. However, Shamanism is also a *spiritual technology* that adjusts and flows to the needs, times and culture in which it is practiced. If enlightenment is the desired outcome, then indeed you may find many resources and tools to support that ultimate goal. The expansive nature of the shamanic mind and energy state can certainly be a vehicle to reach previously unattainable spiritual goals.

Sometimes you come away with a greater awareness of Source energy, believing in a higher power, where once you did not—or maybe you have a different understanding of God and your place in the *Matrix*.

Ayahuasca can help you access the Unified Field of Oneness, where you feel more whole, complete and aware of your true nature. Within this field of transcendent mystery that unifies all wisdom and knowledge, you have and you are, everything already within the realm of intelligent and limitless love.

SPIRITUAL SURGERY

One common explanation of how Ayahuasca heals is through a process of Spiritual Surgery, as the spirits of the plants extract psychological, physical and spiritual causes of dis-ease or imbalances. This could be seen as both literal and metaphoric and is one of the great mysteries of Plant Spirit Healing.

I have often felt these experiences as vibrational, as though I was in a type of advanced healing machine sending healing light rays buzzing through my body from my crown to my feet. I have also felt skillful fingers working on my *chakra* points or rewiring my nervous system. Sometimes, I have had a clear sense of who was performing the *surgeries*, which was often a team of doctors. Occasionally I have received surgery from an animal with a particular skillset. For example, if it is for an area of my body that is particularly sensitive, like my eyes or ears, a doctor frog has come and done surgery with his flicking tongue, skillfully removing energy blockages or repairing nerve damage.

On more than one occasion I have nearly jumped out of my skin when I felt numerous nimble spiritual fingers start their unique healing process on my body—as the doctors come with no warning!

16

THE VINE OF THE SOUL

The nature of rain is the same,
But it makes thorns grow in the marshes
And flowers in the gardens.
~ ARAB PROVERB

The soul is the superconscious and the vine is a creeper that helps me to climb up the tree of my life. I ascend through resistances and limitations, to experience myself from a place of higher awareness, as I rise to the top of the tree's canopy, to see my life from this more expanded state. My soul already knows; my mind can catch up to this heightened state. But my mind and ego can also pull me back down, unless some regular practices keep me aligned with my true nature. The vine naturally curves its way around the trunk and branches, finding the most convenient way on its journey to the light, as this journey is not just a straight shot: it takes perseverance and diligence. I already have the light of conscious awareness inside of me, my ego controls the dimmer switch.

DELUSIONS OF GRANDEUR

In my years of doing this work I have met other ceremony leaders who have many years of training and experience and yet appear to act irresponsibly—without high moral standards and with over-inflated egos. I have sometimes questioned why they have not been healed of these conditions, considering that they have sat in so many Ayahuasca ceremonies.

Occasionally in ceremony, participants may see their inherent self-view with more clarity and in so doing, feel their specialness being validated. They may feel that they are better than others. The ego has a way of bringing in information that reinforces old patterns and beliefs which can be interpreted as Grandmother applauding and approving old behaviors. Everyone who dances with the plant teacher has the power to interpret their own lessons, and if the goal is to support a glorified self-view, then the human trickster mind can help to do that in spades! If they are too attached to their own ego, they may not accept any information they are shown as anything other than validating. Lack of humility can cause ceremony facilitators and attendees to come out of their experience with even more inflated egos than the ones they went in with.

It's also common and happens in many other healing and spiritual traditions—that followers of a particular facilitator will put that person on a pedestal. In most cases, the egotistical facilitator doesn't need any outside help leveraging that view, as they put themselves onto their own pedestal. This may happen with anyone who has narcissistic tendencies. Some can use their Ayahuasca experiences as a strategy to impress on others that they are *special, unique and separate.*

To keep yourself safe, it's best not to put anyone on a pedestal, especially in spiritual work. It's fine to respect and admire someone who is obviously living a life of wisdom and humility—someone who is walking their talk—and to be motivated and influenced by others, in how to live a good life. Always keep in mind that all humans are flawed, and anyone who wants to be worshipped is not going to be a positive influence in their community.

Sometimes delusions of grandeur can cause facilitators or spiritual guides to give you unrealistic expectations, such as: with their help, you can expect to *ascend* in a weekend. This type of self-aggrandizement can be found in places in the US like Sedona, or Mt. Shasta where I used to live and saw this first-hand. Beware of *spiritual chicanery*. It can be found everywhere. This is relevant inside or outside of the Ayahuasca world.

WHAT IS REAL?

The visions that you experience under the influence of Abuela are often metaphoric or symbolic and not literal. Trying to understand the messages held in these visions can sometimes be a source of frustration and it's best to let the inner meanings filter through. One gift you will receive is awareness of how much vaster the nature of mind and the human imagination are, than you may have ever realized before.

When you hear someone say, "Oh, you're just imagining that", it can completely diminish the power of the imaginal process. Our human imagination is one of our most powerful resources. In the Western world, we often consider something *made up* to be less valuable or valid as an experience. But our imaginations actually create our realities.

Ayahuasca has allowed me to access states of expanded imagination that otherwise I would not have access to. Within those states I was shown how to guide others to those expanded places within their subconscious, with emphasis on their own healing and inner peace. She has shown me how to access the path of least resistance to live an optimum life and operate from that place of surrender and power to create an exceptional existence.

When you imagine yourself and who you are, you imagine yourself from the position of "I Am". What and who you are is subjective, based on the imagined beliefs of what "Am" is. "I" is maybe all that is true. "I exist." Then *fill in the blanks* of what that existence means. This is open to your own imaginative creation. The "Am" is constantly in flux, is flexible and malleable and is all you imagine yourself to be.

THE KEYS TO THE KINGDOM

A lot of people come to Ayahuasca ceremonies expecting the ceremony itself to be the change—assuming that Ayahuasca holds the keys to the kingdom. But this is not true. Each individual holds the keys to their own kingdom, beyond the distraction of intrusive thought, limited beliefs and contractive reactions.

We are already everything we want to be and have everything we need. Could it be, these treasures are just buried or obstructed under layers of muck?

CAN AYAHUASCA HELP EVERYONE?

Life is not always a matter of holding good cards
But sometimes
Playing a poor hand well.
~ JACK LONDON

My years of hospice work showed me that the best form of healing I could offer my patients was to help them die in peace and comfort. Some of them and their families only perceived healing as the full remission of their terminal condition. Therefore, they saw the results of my actual healing (helping them die peacefully) as a failure. The same can be true of people seeking Ayahuasca healing: it's not always in the form or with the outcome that you expect.

Some people are born under very hard circumstances, with a lot to bear and they experience an extreme amount of suffering and gut-wrenching trauma. Some of my clients have told me stories that have left me speechless with the amount of tragedy and trauma they've had in their lives. These traumatic experiences can fill them with a sense of deep helplessness and hopelessness. In these cases, sometimes the best form of healing one can expect is to find peace within the challenges: to be able to find hopefulness where there may have only been misery.

During an Ayahuasca journey, the vine might show you why you have experienced what you have and why your coping tools have developed; the plant may also show you how to gain the most from Her teachings and the teachings from your trauma. Ayahuasca can work in mysterious ways: the shift you are asking for may be subtle rather than dramatic. Be open to the medicine and what she shows you.

AYAHUASCA DOES NOT DISCERN

Ayahuasca does not discern how the healing will unfold or how the ceremony itself will unfold. A skillful ceremony leader plays a big part in how the ceremony pans out and the direction in which the energy flows, through their intention and medicine songs. *The clarity of their focus and the resonance of their vibration can determine your experience.* Ayahuasca is not at a set vibration or density, which is why at times you can feel elevated and at other times you can feel really heavy.

Years ago, very early in my Ayahuasca journey, whilst on retreat in the jungle outside of Iquitos, Peru, I was pondering this question: how is it that Ayahuasca can be used by both *Curanderos* (healers) and *Brujos* (sorcerers)? I asked this question to the owner of the retreat center, a North American named Howard Lawler: *Howard, how is it that Ayahuasca, a benevolent spirit, can be used for both benevolent and malevolent ends?* He looked me straight in the eye and simply said "Why do you think She is benevolent?"

That was all I needed to hear and I didn't press any further. I understood that She can be used in whatever way the intention is set. As previously mentioned, Ayahuasca herself does not have intention and does not discern in which way she will activate in the journey. The intention is set primarily by the facilitator and also the individual participants in the session. There is a symbiotic relationship between you and Her.

One would assume that the intention will always be for healing, but that cannot be guaranteed, as the shaman or facilitator may not always have the highest intention for healing. It's important to choose your facilitator and retreat center carefully. Be wary of centers that feel like they're mostly about making money and where they pack participants in like sardines. This is one of the situations where it's in your best interest to get a personal referral, rather than choosing a person or place, based upon a fancy brochure or slick advertising.

WHERE TO DRINK?

There are definitely some situations and precautionary measures that must be taken before joining an Ayahuasca retreat or ceremony. Both participants and facilitators need to practice a high degree of due diligence and investigation. There are many Social Media groups about Ayahuasca, where you can ask questions and find out more information about retreats, etc.

The Ayahuasca business is booming and there has been a huge increase in ceremonies by *weekend shamans* in cities around the globe. You will most likely be okay but you probably won't benefit as much as you would, by going to a venue with authentic and trained facilitators. It's good to ask questions. What is their screening process? What is their reputation? Do you know others who have been there and who reported good experiences?

Maybe you just want ease of access into a ceremonial experience and will take the first thing that comes along? But be aware that most Ayahuasca ceremonies in the West operate outside the law and will most likely be underground. Outside of South and Central America, Ayahuasca is generally considered a controlled substance. You have to do your own soul searching around that. Part of the reason we moved to Ecuador was to openly hold ceremonies, allowing for more safety.

I used to believe that the Ayahuasca experience would always be more powerful in Her homeland—in the jungles of South America, with indigenous maestros or maestras of those lands. Experience has shown me that is not always the case. I have had many transformative and heart centered ceremonies in the US. Setting is important, as mentioned before, as is the knowledge that you are in a safe container and will be well taken care of. Many of my clients have reported major life shifts from ceremonies within the US and elsewhere outside of Latin

America. It's important to be aware of the legal status of Ayahuasca in the region where you wish to participate in ceremony.

AYAHUASCA AND LEGALITY

The Brazilian Ayahuasca Christian churches of Santo Daime and Uniao do Vegetal have legal permission to operate in the US and are more inclined to group participation than the more traditional South American ceremonies. You typically have to be invited to attend their church events.

As a side note, card-carrying Native American ceremonialists can offer plant medicines such as Peyote and Ayahuasca legally, as long as they are held on Indian reservations or in a recognized Native American Church. The Santo Daime and União do Vegetal churches from Brazil, managed to get legal approval to hold ceremonies with plant sacraments, under the same Freedom of Religion Act as the Native American Church in the US. Others operate under this same exemption but as of the time of writing, the DEA is now making arrests and sending Cease and Desist orders to organizations and Ayahuasca churches outside of the Freedom of Religion exemption. The legality of Ayahuasca has been a grey area outside of South America. Organizations like the *Ayahuasca Defense Fund* funded by *ICEERS* (a Spanish non-profit organization, protecting indigenous medicines), can give you updated information about the legal status of Ayahuasca and other plant medicines in your country.

USE DUE DILIGENCE

There is very clearly defined guidance on the internet about how Ayahuasca may interact with pharmaceuticals and herbal stimulants. It's always best to first check with the facilitator or retreat center to know what they suggest. Most of the concern is around SSRI medication that can cause serotonin overload, (known as Serotonin Syndrome), when mixed with the natural serotonin in the sacred brew.

The general precaution is zero tolerance to pharmaceuticals, with a few exceptions, but that is determined on a case-by-case basis.

Ceremony leaders have a responsibility to ensure the safety of everyone in the ceremony. They may have to turn some people away for various reasons. Those with a history of mental illness such as schizophrenia, various forms of psychosis and some personality disorders are usually excluded from ceremony. If someone has a disruptive response to the plant medicine due to a mental health issue or an interaction with medication, it can also be unsafe for other participants and can negatively impact the ceremony for everyone.

It's quite common to fill out a pre-evaluation form before being accepted into ceremony, and participation often requires an interview by the facilitator or their team beforehand. The application form will give dietary guidelines including what is unacceptable in terms of pharmaceutical use and pre-existing physical and mental health concerns, such as high blood pressure and cardiovascular disease. If your health is compromised, it's best to consult a specialist and the retreat center to verify that you will be in a fit state to undergo what can sometimes be a physically arduous experience.

Some of my early Ayahuasca experiences were with indigenous shamans in their homes. They didn't mention any precautions or concerns and I had no pre-ceremony interviews. If you choose to do the same, I suggest you do your own research beforehand. Always use due diligence and recognize that you are ultimately responsible for making the decision to participate.

I have noticed in recent years that retreat centers are offering more and more ceremonies within a seven to ten-day retreat and often with more and more types of medicine. Along with Ayahuasca and Huachuma (San Pedro cactus), they are offering Psilocybin, MDMA, DMT, Cannabis and Bufo. To me, this feels irresponsible and unnecessary. It is a way for them to stand out from the competition and is an element of the consumerist culture which we live in—where you may feel you are getting more *bang for your buck*. I feel it would be difficult to integrate your experiences within this cocktail and could be physically and psychologically dangerous.

IS AYAHUASCA ADDICTIVE?

Ayahuasca itself is definitely not addictive. You do not get a craving if you stop drinking it. Nor have I seen any studies in which anybody struggles to quit drinking Ayahuasca. People can, however, become infatuated with being in the ceremonial experience regularly and get overly attached to the sense of community that surrounds the ceremonial context.

The ceremonial process and the otherworldly nature of the work can be very alluring. It can turn into *spiritual shopping* in which you go from one ceremony to another, or one spiritual group to another looking for answers. In this case, people who are addictive by nature use the ceremonial process as a crutch in the same way as an addictive drug. If you keep doing it without a clear intention for healing, consuming Ayahuasca regularly can be similar to chasing rainbows.

You will find that the more regularly you drink, the less medicine you need to drink to obtain similar results. It would be unusual for anyone to build a tolerance to Ayahuasca where they need more and more to feel an effect.

SORCERY

There is nothing that causes so much suffering
As the lies we tell ourselves.

~ DR. BESSEL VAN DE KOLK

Sorcery is an ancient profession that is still practiced widely
in the Amazon regions, both with and without using plant
medicines. As mentioned previously, Ayahuasca is not discerning about how Her energy is used. She can be used for good or
for evil at the discretion of the user.

The indigenous cultures of South America, as well as most
indigenous cultures worldwide, hold to the *Animistic* belief that
everything is alive, everything has consciousness and everything has a supernatural essence. These cultures also tend to
have inherited beliefs in spiritual interference being connected
to health, luck, relationships, financial abundance, etc. They
believe strongly that evil energies can be projected onto individuals and communities to seriously impact the physical and
psychological well-being of the person/s to whom the sorcery is
being directed.

Mostly, sorcery is performed by the sorcerer or brujo, due
to their own or their paying client's *celos* (jealousy), or *envidiar*

(envy), which is the predominant reason for negative intentions on another. Because of the modern-day interest in Ayahuasca tourism, millions of dollars are being introduced into places like Iquitos, Peru, where there is much competition between retreat centers and individuals trying to maximize their incomes and influence. This has caused a spike in *daño* (harm) or *mal de ojo* (evil eye), directed at competing shamans. Once a healer has been influenced to go to the dark side, there is no going back. They can no longer be a trusted healer.

I hear of shamans in the Ayahuasca world and elsewhere, who perform spiritual attacks with metaphysical poisoned darts, sometimes called *virotes*, that are shot energetically from one shaman to another. In these cultures, bad health is pretty much always attributed to some form of daño and requires an actual Shaman skilled in *incantos* (protection prayers or songs), to help reverse the energetic cause of the evil intent.

In one of my first Ayahuasca ceremonies with Maestro Pedro, a Bruja (witch) and her not-so-bright son were present. There were only the four of us. She told me that she needed help with releasing the negative energy she had accrued by doing sorcery, which was affecting not just she and her family (she pointed to her son and shrugged in frustration), but her neighbors as well.

After she and her son left the next morning, Pedro told me that to be a sorcerer is a lot easier than being a healer, as the discipline and training is far longer, more intense and more demanding for healers. Keeping high moral and ethical standards require strong discipline.

I feel I keep myself aligned with my trainings and after my experience with Bob (recounted below), I vowed never to wish harm to anyone for anything, no matter how frustrated or angry I became with someone.

There is a market in Cusco, Peru known as the Witches' market where one can buy paraphernalia for casting spells or for making offerings to the ancestors or spirit realm. Things such as llama fetus and herbal concoctions, different scents and lead castings, feathers and candles of all shapes, sizes and colors are but a few things readily available. You can buy soaps or perfumes to bring about miraculous abundance or to repel your enemy. The world of sorcery is a good living for many and you see brujos (sorcerers) advertising their services with signs, saying things like: "meet your lover", "get a 3-day erection—guaranteed", "get rich", "overwhelm the competition", and "kill your neighbor". (Yes, I did actually see that!). The Shamans whom I trust, never advertise in this way—they rely purely on word of mouth.

Bob

Years ago, when I first started on my path as a healer, I was working full-time during the day as a furniture maker and then offering healing work on evenings and weekends. A fellow co-worker whom I will call Bob, had terrible anger issues and would sometimes vent his anger at me. I really liked my job and the beautiful furniture I was commissioned to make, even though at times Bob's explosive temper could ruin my day. This situation was exacerbated when I was promoted to Foreman, because I had only been working at the company a few years, whereas Bob had worked there for two decades. He did not take it well!

I knew that the only way he would leave would be if he got badly injured.

One morning after yet another outburst directed at me, I secretly wished him harm. Within a minute, I heard a shout coming from his area of the workshop and saw him standing there with his face contorted in pain. Bob had cut off the top of his finger with an electric router—a very dangerous tool if not used properly—and he certainly knew how to use it properly! I knew in that moment that more than likely I caused his accident with the focus of my intention.

Realizing my responsibility, I drove Bob to the hospital to get his finger fixed and fortunately he was able to return to work a few days later. I decided to leave the company after that incident to focus full time on my healing work. This event was a huge lesson for me and one that I have heeded ever since; I NEVER wish harm.

NEVER WISH HARM

After that experience, I recognized that I had developed a strong capacity to focus my attention and that this focus could be damaging to myself and to others, if I used it unscrupulously. On the bright side, this showed me that if I could cause harm this quickly and effectively just by focusing on it, then I could similarly bring about immediate well-being or healing.

In the next chapter I explore why the human experience can be so challenging and why our struggle can drive many of us to seek out this powerful elixir from the Amazon Basin. Why aren't we just naturally happy and healthy?

THE HARD PATH

The worst that happens to you
Can be the best thing for you,
If you don't let it get the best of you.
~ ANONYMOUS

We Homo sapiens seem hard wired for negative and restrictive reactions, even though we know that it causes suffering. We often play small without knowing it, even though we may feel we are playing big. It feels safe. It feels familiar.

In my work, I focus initially on the psycho-spiritual relationship of limiting behaviors, actions and beliefs. This helps me to trace the originating cause of the energetic components of a condition that I work on next. Some of the ways I work in this realm are explained in Part III.

I find that most people who come to me have core issues that affect their whole sense of self. These are:

- Not feeling safe in the world; meaning not feeling safe in the body.
- Not feeling worthy to be loved, or essentially—not lovable.

Both of these conditions lead to a restrictive way of living. People develop many negative, fearful or diminished beliefs about themselves, often leading to associated physical ailments or dis-ease.

So, a lot of my focus with them is:

- Helping them to feel safe.
- Teaching them how to love themselves.

Our minds and bodies crave that which is familiar, even if it is self-destructive or self-sabotaging, such as being in an abusive relationship like the one you perhaps witnessed between your parents. The effects of self-sabotage can be compelling, as in being judgmental or hyper controlling because you want to create the illusion that the world is as you believe it to be. This can allow you to feel safe and self-assured. Holding onto the familiarity of those painful reactions must feel better than releasing them. After all, why do you keep replaying the same old dramas?

Our brains can get stuck in patterns. The subconscious is wired to do this as a way to allow our conscious brain to focus on new situations. When our brain decides that a certain thought or behavior pattern gives us some benefit, the sub-conscious becomes conditioned accordingly and we no longer have to spend mental energy choosing the pattern over and over again.

The human brain also has a negativity bias, which is a natural tendency to remember negative experiences more than positive ones, as though it's hardwired to be attracted to the bad and less likely to focus on the good. Changing this tendency takes mental training and a change in belief patterns.

We are thinking beings. Our brains are always looking for interesting things to process. Our bodies are more activated and more stimulated by negative memories. Positive experiences generally are softer on the body and don't leave such a dominant imprint. They don't engage the body or mind in the same way and our minds love to be engaged.

In addition to remembering negative experiences more clearly, people tend to weigh negative memories more heavily than they do positive events. When our Boss says something mean to us at work, we tend to remember that incident more clearly—and be more affected by it—than when our co-worker compliments us on our work presentation.

Furthermore, we often have an underlying belief that something will go wrong. This can be more pronounced after a traumatic event—whether it be an assault, accident, loss of a loved one or a breakup. It often involves thoughts that are in some way related to the initial event, such as being anxious when strangers pass us on the sidewalk after we've experienced being mugged. The brain is reacting to these triggers to prepare us psychologically and emotionally for further traumatic situations. This often causes us to have an overreaction of responses or emotions.

You may wish that your brain didn't react this way, but your brain is doing its job keeping you safe from muggers. All of these mental and emotional strategies have developed from our primal desire to survive and to maintain the human species. Most of it is now irrelevant for the survival of the species yet remains directly related to your sense of feeling safe or un-safe. Feeling unsafe causes your nervous system to react through triggers and tensions, which then causes you to resist, rather than flow with life. The pain this creates is hard to live with as it produces unhappiness and negative states of mind.

Many books have been written about the human mind and its many afflictions and the underlying causes of those afflictions.

I don't need to harp on about what they are. A better use of your valuable time is to get straight into how you can live a happier, more self-loving and safe existence. It's not hard. Living an unhappy, self-loathing and fear filled existence is hard. The rest of this book shows you how to gain self-mastery over negative, contractive and tense states.

PART III

The Easy Path

SELF MASTERY

The Path to happiness is an easy path, in fact the easiest path.
The Path to misery is hard and includes stress and tension.
Why not take the easy path—the Path of Self Mastery!

~ A.F.W.

The first part of this book speaks to my own path of moving away from deep depression and developing expanded states of awareness in the process. It was ultimately a beautiful path, that alleviated so many of my self-diminishing patterns. I recognized that every step of the way gave me a deep teaching about gaining self-mastery in life. The simple teachings of the maestros I wrote about in Part II, about *dominating* my doubts and self-sabotaging behaviors helped me to recognize I had the power to create my own destiny and regulate my mental and emotional states. With the help of Ayahuasca, I learnt to strengthen my character and my spirit to create clear, non-negotiable boundaries with myself and with others.

Part III is some of what I have learnt on my apprenticeship: how to help people heal. It has been quite a journey and one in which Ayahuasca and San Pedro cactus have been my greatest teachers. I learnt numerous healing techniques from humans but it is the Plant Teachers—the Master Teachers, who taught me how to maneuver through the subtle layers of the subconscious, to perform energy extractions and to shift density. These teachings have had the greatest impact on my clients' lives and on my own life.

If you learn some of these techniques, you will be on a solid path if you too are a healer, or if you wish to gain more control over your own well-being.

Accessing the subtle realms to work with the subconscious is one of the greatest gifts Ayahuasca has given me. I can only work to the depth that I myself can go and I continue to strive to access deeper levels, to help my clients heal to those same depths.

THE SWEET SPOT

You can't touch love,
But you can feel the sweetness it pours
Into everything.
~ ANNE SULLIVAN MACY

Ayahuasca tends to have a particular rhythm. For those who have experienced Her, you know that there is an initial *high* that can last from one to four hours. This is the point where most visions and intense other worldly experiences happen, and then the energy starts to smooth out. Within that, there is an alignment of body, mind and spirit where energy starts to flow at an optimum level for healing: it is the place of homeostasis. This is where I can enter the subtle realms to go deep into the energy field of my client. I call it *The Sweet Spot*.

In the Sweet Spot I trace a line through the portal of my client's emotions to clear the stuck energy associated with core limiting beliefs, that developed out of a traumatic experience in their life. It is a gentle process and I encourage my client to surrender and open to what is happening.

I do not need to use Ayahuasca to help transform my client's life although, She can hold the most powerful potential for transformation. I also help my clients access the optimal state for healing through guided imagery and breathwork.

ENTERING THE SWEET SPOT

The causes of dis-ease in the body and mind are stress or fear or tension-based beliefs, or reactions. These reactions cause anxiety, depression, self-loathing, anger, hatred, pain, resentment, psychological imbalance, PTSD, etc. In these reactions you are experiencing states of hypervigilance or you are in survival mode.

Every negative experience of your body or mind has a tension associated with it. Usually, the tension precedes the reaction of the associated triggers. This is also where illness and imbalances dwell. Expanded states of conscious awareness are achieved through relaxation and they are happy, open, loving, confident states. In fact, these states are impossible to experience unless you are relaxed.

A relaxed state expands conscious awareness. A tense state contracts conscious awareness.

Soften your body and your breath and your reactions soften, allowing you to enter an expanded state. Notice how peaceful this is. This also allows your body to rest from the rigors of tension.

You cannot be happy and tense. In the same way—you can't be angry and relaxed. Try it! Relax and try to feel angry. Tense up and try to feel peaceful. Try saying "I am angry" when you are relaxing. It doesn't work. Try saying "I feel happy and peaceful" when you tense up your entire body. It's a very simple exercise which helps to emphasize my process. Thanks to Serge Kahili King and his book *Urban Shaman*, for clarification on this process.

When you relax and expand, you can experience love. When you tense, you shut down the capacity to do so. Reflect on all the times you have gotten mad at a partner or a child and then you wanted to just run out of the room. You shut down to feelings of love. You know that you love this person but you probably are not feeling it in that moment. Afterwards when you have a coming together that allows you to release the tension, all of a sudden you are feeling the love again!

Simply put, the sweet spot is attained by entering a state of effortlessness. However, it doesn't mean you just lie there and blank out. You must have an intention for the healing process to start, to activate the body's healing intelligence and then you create step by step, the conditions that are required for healing. At this point you get out of the way.

The Sweet Spot is really sweet—you know it when you're there because it feels so amazing!

ENTERING THE DEATH ZONE

As a hospice volunteer veteran, or *Death Doula*, I have also witnessed hundreds of people moving through what is known as the *end stage*, where they move into the last stage of their physically embodied life. This state often has a lot of tension that emanates from the pain, anger and fear of leaving the physical body. I also witnessed erratic breathing—the chest rising with a big inhale and an extended period before the exhale and then a delayed next inhale. Often the patient stares blankly into space.

At some point, the body goes through a physiological shift governed by a Divine Intelligence, as the body relaxes and prepares for what is to come. In this alchemical space between life and death, the body aligns itself for the transitional phase. It releases tension. Breathing becomes soft and relaxed so that the spirit can leave the body. At this point the physical vessel is no longer needed and the body releases its last exhale—its last autonomous action of this life.

I liken this moment to the sweet spot of healing, but unlike in the dying process, when the body releases all tension to transcend beyond itself—

The Sweet Spot of healing allows the body to transcend into a more vibrant version of itself.

20

RELAXATION AND THE
SIMPLE WAY

Simplicity is the ultimate sophistication.
~ LEONARDO DA VINCI

Relaxation alone will not transform your life. It's also important to introduce new ideas and feelings into your body by using your imagination, your breath, your trust, your intention and your confidence.

You can focus on the fact you are being reactive, by bringing your attention to it. Then you breathe into it. Take long, soft inhales and relaxed exhales. You will eventually find the sweet spot, that is your natural state of ease—pure and beautiful. Everything flows from that point. The mind leads and the body follows.

The body sensations during relaxation benefits the whole body plus the conscious and subconscious mind. I consider the path to relaxation as the absence of doing. To relax, it's important to have the intention to relax and then surrender to relaxation. The body knows what to do when the conditions of mindful relaxation are presented to it.

tension = effort   relaxation = effortlessness

The intention to relax precedes the process of relaxation. It would be hard to relax if you didn't have the desire to relax. So, relaxing within this process is a conscious relaxation, whereas stress is usually un-conscious. However, the optimum state of wellbeing also has an additional quality to it—the intention to heal.

The beautiful thing in working with a healer who can help you enter this state of *healing relaxation*, is that the healer *also* has the desire and intention for you to heal.

Imagine you are receiving *Reiki* (energy healing) and both you and the Reiki practitioner have a deep desire and intention for you to heal. You have doubled the capacity for you to receive a healing outcome, because now there are two of you involved. The healer with the volitional and intentional desire for healing and you the recipient, with an open receptive desire for healing—allowing for the circuit of healing to be amplified.

When you are at a heightened vibrational state you are entering a state of healing. Viruses and bacteria thrive on lower vibrational states—it attracts them, as they themselves come from these lower states. Therefore, when you raise your vibrational state, viruses and bacteria can't thrive, can't exist. You become healthier and free of the parasitic influences that feed off your life force.

Relaxed states: Happy: Healing states
Tense states: Unhappy: Stressful: Non-Healing states

Once you make a shift towards healing and you repeat the process a few times on your own, you will deepen your healing. At some point, the depth of your healing will be stronger than the cause of ill health and you will continue to move on the path of transformation.

But first, ask yourself:

- Am I ready to change?
- Am I ready to build my spiritual strength and character?
- Do I want to elevate myself above my limiting beliefs?
- Am I worthy to be happy?
- Am I willing to invest time and money to explore the possibilities that are open to me?
- Am I willing to love all the parts of myself that I rejected?

If you answered NO to the above questions, you are choosing a path of resistance, which is the Hard Path.

If you answered YES to these questions, you are ready to learn the Easy Path. In fact, you are already on that path, first because you bought this book. Second because you got this far in the book and third and most importantly, now saying YES—I am ready to change. Healing is the easiest thing you can do. When you are in a state of full mental, emotional, physical and spiritual ease, you are in a state of healing.

HOMEOSTASIS, HEALTH AND HEALING

Homeostasis refers to equilibrium: when living things function with minimal resistance to their natural state, they maintain stable conditions within themselves necessary for their survival. When you are stressed or hold tension in the body, you put yourself out of a harmonious relationship to the homeostatic state.

The body knows how to heal itself if the right conditions are presented. The body's healing needs to be supported with healthy food and lifestyle but, if you don't deal with the originating causes of tension (energy blocks), then no amount of good eating is going to get you back to physical or mental balance. It is important for the body to have a stable energetic environment for cells to function correctly.

I teach breathing techniques to my clients to relax them and to allow them to enter a state of flow. I then use Reiki or a combination of Reiki, breathwork and simple *hypnotherapeutic* techniques, to guide them into the subtle realms.

THE POWER OF REIKI ENERGY HEALING

Reiki is known as Divinely Guided Universal Life Force Energy—a simple and powerful technique that enhances the relaxation response.

When quickly relaxed by a Reiki practitioner channeling Reiki, the client will enter a state of calm, peace and safety that allows for the balancing of mind, body and spirit, thereby enhancing the body's capacity to heal. I first trained in Reiki because I wanted to help the hospice patients where I volunteered.

The first time I used Reiki at hospice after taking an introductory Reiki class, I witnessed my aged patient go from a state of tension, noticeable through his end stage breathing (known as the *Death Rattle*), to one of peace within a couple of minutes. This allowed him to transition peacefully and pain free. I was immediately sold on its effects and now I use Reiki in all of my healing sessions. I have taught hundreds of Reiki students how to facilitate this simple and powerful process. I love teaching Reiki!

*Reiki is a powerful foundational tool for your
Spiritual Toolbox, as it can be used in any healing practice.
I recommend that you learn Reiki as a way to quickly
enhance your body's healing capacity and to help heal others.*

Christine's Story

Years ago, Christine, a 40-year-old lesbian, came to me because she and her partner were trying to have a child, and despite 2 previous in-vitro fertilizations, they had not been successful. Due to cost and health concerns, they decided to give it one last try. Understandably, Christine was nervous about it. I saw very quickly that the cause of the failed pregnancies was tension. I could see where the energy was blocked throughout the previous treatments, due to the fear and doubt she held in her body. I then foresaw how the energy was now going to flow throughout this last attempt to birth a child. I even foresaw the birth of twins.

Initially, I gave Reiki to Christine to calm her nerves and then proceeded to offer her a shamanic healing that I sent forward in time, from the point of fertilization through the whole pregnancy, seeing her relaxed during the whole process.

She and her partner are now proud parents of healthy 15-year-old twin boys.

RELAXATION AND SLEEP

The body needs sleep to recuperate after a hard day at work. Sleep promotes the healing of body and mind by releasing hormones that are necessary to repair damaged tissues and blood vessels. Sleep also comes with dreams that can offer wisdom and insights, but it can also bring anxiety or fear-based stress.

I have found that intentional relaxation techniques, along

with guided imagery or shamanic journeying, can actually elicit a more pronounced healing outcome than just sleep alone. Sleep alone is not enough as the client probably sleeps every night but, still comes to me for healing deeply rooted conditions that continue to distress them.

THE PATH OF LEAST RESISTANCE

If you want to quit smoking,
Stop putting cigarettes in your mouth.

~ MICHAEL SINGER

So, what is the path of least resistance? If you have behaviors, thoughts or actions that no longer serve you and you want to stop doing them—then STOP doing them! When you stop, you have stopped resisting stopping.

Simple, right?! What could be a more effective way to change your life than to stop repeating patterns that are self-destructive? You haven't stopped because you are getting something from the behaviors. Maybe you didn't realize that you had the power to move on?

It can take you one minute to decide that the Hard Path is no longer for you. You can take a circuitous route of experiencing life before you realize that the old way doesn't work, so why not try a new strategy?

The hard path was your teacher. The hard path gave you your chops and experience. Now it's time to use that experience to develop mastery in another form of living: the path of least resistance. Nothing has been wasted. You change when you are ready to change and not before. Some of us arrive at this decision early in life and some of us aren't ready until later. I didn't discover the simple path until I was in my 40's.

21

RESISTANCE AND FLOW

In a gentle way
You can shake the world.

~ GANDHI

Resistance usually starts in your head. Here are some thoughts you have probably had in your life:

- But it's too simple.—Resistance
- How can I transform patterns I've had for so long?—Resistance
- Will I be able to do it?—Resistance
- I can't do it.—Resistance
- Am I doing it right?—Resistance
- I can only go so deep.—Resistance
- I fail at everything.—Resistance
- What if it goes wrong?—Resistance

Resistance is a *thinking* generated state.

- It's so Easy.—Flow
- It feels amazing.—Flow

- I feel peaceful.—Flow
- It's so gentle.—Flow
- It feels safe.—Flow
- I feel so embodied.—Flow
- It's so comfortable.—Flow
- I feel happy.—Flow

Flow is a *feeling* generated state.
Resistance is restrictive. Flow is expansive.

PEACEFUL AND AMAZING EXERCISE

If you identify a resistance-based experience, remind yourself you are in your head. No need to be hard on yourself. Learn to be soft. Laugh at it. "Oh yeah, I'm in my head!"

Let yourself notice your hands and your feet, notice your breath and above all, notice how peaceful and amazing your breath feels. Say out loud how peaceful and amazing it feels to breathe. If it doesn't feel peaceful and amazing, then you are experiencing resistance to feeling peaceful and amazing. What can you do in this moment to feel peaceful and amazing? This is your work. Peaceful and amazing are right on the other side of resistance—I guarantee you. The deeper you go into peaceful and amazing, the deeper you go into yourself and the deeper you go into healing.

Everything is relevant for the evolution of your soul.

This is the Easy Path. This way is about finding the path of least resistance inside yourself. It is about opening up neurological and nervous system pathways to reduce stress and lower muscular and nervous system resistance. When you do this practice, energy can flow through your body, to be used in any way your body chooses. It can invigorate your body, your mind and your emotions. In the state of minimized resistance, you can manifest anything you choose to focus upon. With minimized resistance you have maximized energy.

As in Tai Chi or Chi Kung, you direct the flow of life force energy. On this easy path, you use self-mastery qualities of awareness and surrender. *By allowing miniscule inner adjustments of surrender, you let go of reactivity, control, self-sabotage and triggers, to forge new pathways of softness, gentleness and awareness.*

KEEPING IT SIMPLE

You may think . . .

You mean, I have struggled all these years unnecessarily? This Alan guy is treating all this too simplistically. How can this help me to heal years of negativity? I can't accept that!

It sounds too easy because you are expecting it to be hard and painful to resolve your internal conflicts. Isn't that funny? It's almost miraculous how the easy path can shift your life, often in dramatic ways and YOU become the healer of your own health and wellness.

I repeat, healing is very simple: that is my maxim. By now you have a sense of me. You have an idea of my journey and my ideas around healing. So, trust it, if you will. This is not about thinking. Thinking gets you in trouble: this is about feeling. About moving deeper into your feelings and honoring all of them. Hopefully you can laugh at how simple it is. You will be amazed at the shifts you will experience.

When you are with me in person or online, I guide you through this process. I intuitively sense where the most beneficial journey will lead you and then at the precise moment when I feel you are ready, I will perform a *Shamanic Energy Extraction*—the way that Ayahuasca taught me. As such, Ayahuasca is participating in the process.

Wellness is not a privilege—it is your birthright.

Learn to live simply. Make choices that support the simple approach to life and well-being. Spend more time connecting to nature because you are nature. Learn to reconnect with and to yourself. Get off social media and stop ruminating on media generated or societal idealized versions of yourself, otherwise you will be turning *gold into lead.*

Step into your bliss by following your passions. If you keep hating your job or aspects of your life, you are filling your life with hopelessness and despair. Move out of the fear-based comfort zone you created for yourself. Step up. Take risks.

Shifts can take up to six months after a healing session with me to manifest fully and are usually noticed in hindsight, where they can't be denied any longer. Clients often report back to me: "I don't react the same way as I used to!", "I don't have the pain in my knee anymore; I completely forgot about it!"

LIFE DOESN'T HAVE TO BE THAT HARD

When there is something within you
That moves in the right direction,
It creates its own discipline.
~ ANTHONY DE MELLO

You are the one who makes life hard on yourself. At some level you made that choice, whether it's because you developed body shame, unworthiness, hypervigilant behaviors, depression or anxiety. You hold these thoughts, beliefs or reactions in your body and mind. You are the one who must take full responsibility. Your resistance to living openly and peacefully causes your greatest problems and hardships.

People who are stuck in their heads and who take themselves too seriously all the time tend to walk the path of difficulty. I have never seen people smile or laugh as much as I have with the Tibetan monks and nuns. Even in the face of such incredible adversity, they have a brightness about them that comes from deep within their souls. If they focused solely on their problems, they would be miserable. It's their choice to be happy.

UNDERLYING NEGATIVE BELIEFS
UPHOLD UNHEALTHY BEHAVIORS

Your choices are so wrapped up in a particular belief system that you have to look outside your conditioning to get clarity. This can be scary. Therein lies a dilemma for those who are fundamentally attached to a specific conditioned reality (which is most of us). But, who would you be without this condition, situation, or behavior? This addiction?

Ask yourself:

- Am I not allowing myself to release this addiction because it means I would have to deal with the underlying cause?
- Am I afraid that I'm not strong enough?
- Am I afraid that I will fail and be hard on myself for being a failure?
- Am I so used to failing, that it feels crazy to expect anything else?
- Am I worthy?

Even small behavior shifts create momentum. Think of a stick floating in a stream that continues to move with the flow of the water, even if it gets held up on a snag every now or then. When we commit to making small, consistent changes, they create their own current of transformation in our lives, until eventually making healthier choices becomes easier.

Who you are today is a result of your subconscious memory having tracked and stacked all the experiences and influences of your life.

THE POWER OF CHOICE

When someone comes to me with a chronic condition, I listen carefully to hear whether the client is really committed to ending this run of sickness or disharmony.

One of the first things I wish to understand from my client is whether they are willing to do what is required to change whatever condition or situation they're struggling with. Are they really willing to let go of the beliefs, habits and behaviors that underly the condition? You may believe you are willing to change because you think you would be better off without a particular addiction, but your words or body language can reveal something else.

I had a client Ann, who had developed terrible anger issues that she traced back to the immense amount of physical and emotional abuse she received as a child, from her father. We went into the gentle processes I use but she would not accept that the gentle approach would help her with her issues. She said "It's too soft, I need something harder." It made me think of Newton's 3rd Law of Motion—*for every action (force) there is an equal and opposite reaction.* She wanted an opposite force which would have created an immense amount of friction and resistance, whereas to allow herself to soften *through* the force of her anger, would be the most beneficial for her. Unfortunately, because she resisted this process, I was unable to do my Shamanic Energy Extraction. We agreed that I was not the best fit for her. I obviously can't help everyone.

When people are less than fully committed to making a life change, they might have a hidden belief that they will not be *able* to change. A half-hearted commitment is not a clear choice for change. A clear choice sparks confidence and commitment behind both the decision and the subsequent action, thereby allowing for more success with the outcome. Sometimes when

I ask clients if they are ready to change, they say "yes?"—like it's a question rather than a statement.

YES OR NO EXERCISE

Ask yourself if you are committed to changing aspects of your life that don't work for you any longer. If saying "YES," notice the expression of the word. I recommend saying it out loud, with a clear confident "YES!" Practice it. Can you feel "YES" in your whole body? Practice saying "NO!" too. Say NO to situations in your life that you will no longer allow. "NO!" is a powerful choice to make and express, especially around boundary setting.

In my teens and 20's, I made the decision to be depressed. I wasn't conscious of that decision—but nobody else made it for me! It gave me a reason to stay small and hidden away.

If I had continued living the life I had been living, why would I expect my life to not continue being hard? In making the choice to live, I had to make supporting choices that would allow me to change my belief systems. There was no clearly defined path to doing that, just a trust that the choices I was going to make, guided by Amantane, would somehow lead me from a path of depression into happiness.

I often ask clients: *Does maintaining your unhealthy condition or situation, benefit you in some way?*

23

THE POWER OF WORDS

A session with Ayahuasca
Is equivalent
To 10 years of therapy.

~ ANONYMOUS

The above quote can be seen on a variety of websites that I have come across over the years. I have no idea of its origin and it is a claim that cannot be verified. I do not wish to dispute it. I imagine it is referring to the potential for transformation one might receive from a powerful Ayahuasca session. It does however, beg the question—why would someone continue therapy over many years, with negligible results? Do they go into traditional psychotherapy not expecting any shift? Are they content to ruminate about their issues with no expectation of a beneficial outcome?

I mean no disrespect to respectable and highly trained therapy professionals, as I know they help many people through crises. I have had many licensed therapists as clients over the years. They have their own views about the efficacy of their profession.

On the other hand, if you go into an Ayahuasca session or a shamanic healing session with the agreed-on goal that you are looking for a powerful transformation—quickly—the energy and the focus of that intentionality will often result in a noticeable shift. I have seen this with myself and with many clients. My healing sessions start with the question: *Are you ready to change?* When I get a clear "Yes", I follow up with something like: *Great! Let's get this done!*

I continue by asking about their story and about what might be considered *high impact events* in their lives. We only talk about this once.

The instructions after that are all focused towards quick, significant transformations using words that support the desired changes. Words such as *transformation, potential, hope, light, exceptional,* contain power, while words like *trauma, wounds, triggers, negativity, PTSD, helplessness or limiting beliefs*, are energetically diminishing. When both the client and the healer set the target clearly and powerfully, a change is likely to occur. I have a long track record which proves this to be true.

I am not interested in long-term professional relationships with clients—no offense intended! We may become friends—which is a wonderful benefit of my work—but I'm completely focused on helping you heal—quickly!

Lise's Story

Many years ago, when I first began offering healing work, I didn't really know what I was doing. I hadn't received any formal training; it was just training from my heart, my life experiences and some early teachings from Michael Harner and Ayahuasca.

One of my fellow hospice volunteers, Lise, had been diagnosed with Stage 3 ovarian cancer throughout her abdomen, liver and diaphragm. She was told it was a very aggressive form of cancer and she had started treatments of chemotherapy. Her partner at the time—a medical doctor, was not very positive about her long-term survival and consequently, she was scared and anxious. As a friend, I offered to go to her house on a regular basis and give her healing sessions and emotional support. The evening of the first session, I looked her in the eyes and said:

How would you like to completely get rid of this cancer!?

I saw a flicker in her eyes; the sound of these words offered her a new possibility that she hadn't considered before—a hope that she certainly wasn't receiving from the doctors nor her boyfriend. I knew from that spark in her eyes, the potential of this new possibility was being actualized in that split-second. It wasn't something I had planned. The words were guided by a force outside of myself.

I continued weekly sessions with Lise for a few months, supporting her emotional and spiritual needs with words of positivity and hope. I made sure my language was always powerfully strengthening her well-being.

Fifteen years later, Lise is thriving and cancer free. She attests that her sessions with me were a significant factor as to why she is still alive. I know that my initial words of hope along with my care and concern for her well-being, were all part of the healing she received. I learnt from that experience the profound healing power of words supported by the healing power of love.

SPEAKING YOUR TRUTH EXERCISE

This exercise shows the power of the words you use and the instant response of your feeling state which responds to positive and uplifting words, as well as to negative, diminishing words. Your body's nervous system instantly matches the words and the significance that those words have for you, whether you realize it or not. Speak your truth. How can you set clear boundaries if you can't speak your truth? Similarly, you cannot live your truth if you cannot speak it. Be vigilant and mindful of the words you use. Words are very powerful; they become manifest. Your words are part of your embodied self. What you say you become.

Start by talking to yourself. Speak out loud anything positive or loving you wish to say about and to yourself, that you haven't said out loud before. Let positive energy be expressed through your words. Remember, it is you talking to YOU. You being honest with YOU.

Continue speaking with one hand on your heart to focus your intention there. Use these sentences as a guide:

"Something I've never told you is . . . "

"What I am angry about is . . . "

"When I was young, I felt afraid because of. . . . "

"My heart closed down because. . . . "

"I've always wanted to tell you how much I. . . . "

"I forgive you for. . . . "

As you speak, go into your heart feelings. See if you can soften those feelings. Feel the impact that the words spoken out loud have on your body or feeling state. Take your time. Transformation happens through the whole body, not just the head. The deeper you feel the meaning of the words, the deeper the transformational opportunity. You cannot think your way into a deeper state, you can only surrender into a deeper state. Surrender has a feeling associated with it: can you sense the feeling of surrender?

Words spoken out loud are a portal into deeper feeling and emotional states. The throat chakra tends to be the first chakra I work on with energy release, as it has the most significant and fundamental impact on the client.

An energetically blocked throat chakra causes looping energy patterns and associated negative looping thoughts—which keep you stuck in the head. When the throat chakra is cleared by speaking your truth, the energy can flow down to the heart and then the rest of the body. Thoughts can be more heart centered and embodied.

You will notice how expressing affirming loving words, your body experiences loving affirming feelings. The opposite is also true. Pay attention to the words you say or think to yourself.

Go out there into the world and start speaking your truth to family and friends. Challenge yourself. Be honest. Write a list of everyone you want to have a heart centered conversation with and work your way through it. The fear of confrontation or truth talking is just resistance. Talk through it. Talk with feeling. Speak from the heart. Nobody can deny your feelings, but they can resist your thoughts; often when you speak from your head it might trigger their own wounds. Encourage them to go into their feelings. That's where transformation happens.

SETTING CLEAR BOUNDARIES

Do you ever think:

- I'm not even sure my opinions matter.
- Why does that person keep doing that even though I've asked them nicely not to?
- Why do I never seem to be taken seriously?
- Why doesn't anyone listen to me?

Such thoughts indicate that you are not setting clear boundaries. This is related to low self-worth and self-doubt, both of which diminish personal power. To set a clear boundary, you must understand what is required.

It's hard to set clear boundaries when you are not clear yourself. Some people set boundaries with shouting and angry outbursts, thinking that if they can shout louder than the other person, they win! Set clear boundaries with yourself from a place that is assertive and confident. Take back your personal authority and operate from a place of greater self-respect.

Archetypal beliefs such as *I Am a Victim* limit your capacity to engage your spiritual power—where authentic clear boundaries emanate from. Clear boundaries with others first start with setting clear, non-negotiable boundaries with yourself. If in setting those boundaries you are influenced in any way by fears that you are not good enough, or not worthy to speak your truth—then that is where you set the boundaries from.

GETTING CLEAR

First, recognize the difference between doubt and confidence. From an energetic perspective: doubt is an energy inhibiter and confidence is an energy catalyzer.

If you say, "I don't like it when you do such and such," whilst shuffling your feet, speaking from your head, breathing in short breaths, wringing your hands and avoiding eye contact—how will you be perceived by the person you're speaking to? Probably not very well. That is The Doubter.

How about if you look them directly in the eye without flinching, stand up tall with your shoulders back, breathe deeply from your core, and clearly and slowly say: "I do NOT like it when you do such and such." It will land very differently.

This is the Confident one.

BE A WARRIOR (NOT A WORRIER) EXERCISE

It's more powerful to do this standing up. This is a statement of action, a statement of being. Speak without umm-ing and aaah-ing. Speak with power.

Put your hands in the air above your head, take a deep breath, push your chest out and shoulders back. Plant your feet firmly on the ground and state the decree below with as confident a voice as you can muster:

"I (your birth name or your spiritual name) am a Warrior of Light and I hereby decree that from this point on, I will live in my power, guided by my heart, my intuition and my belief in myself, to only live from a place of confidence, strength, and courage. I will live my best life with good health, happiness and full personal sovereignty. For I AM . . . name".

Take a deep breath and with your hands still above your head, notice how your cells are vibrating. Next—with your hands on your heart and your eyes closed whilst breathing deeply, take some time to integrate the shift.

Well done.

The words above are suggestions. Choose your own. Again, it's more powerful to state what you wish to embody and not what you want to let go of. Do this regularly. Also do it looking at yourself in a mirror. You may notice that your face changes over time. Also do it in front of someone else. It is powerful to have someone witness your truth. Take turns.

I use this process in group retreats to help participants step fully into the embodied higher version of themselves, witnessed by the group. After each participant's turn, I will often have the person to the speaker's left (this person is a witness) stand in front of them, put a hand on each of the speaker's shoulders, and look them directly in the eyes. The witness then says: "I see you. I hear you. I feel you. I am here." This lets the speaker know that he or she was heard and is supported.

The whole group cheers, shakes rattles and makes whooping sounds to help lift the vibration. We finish by giving each other a hug.

24

EMBODYING AND SHAPE-SHIFTING

It is better to live your destiny imperfectly
Than to live an imitation of
Somebody else's life with perfection.

~ BHAGAVAD-GITA

We do embodiment and *shape-shifting* processes all the time without realizing it. What we embody we are: any energy or belief we have about ourselves, we do not only believe, we become. Another way of saying this is: we develop personality traits or behaviors known as *archetypes*.

Swiss psychiatrist Carl Jung believed that archetypes exist in the collective unconscious and manifest in our personalities in different ways based on our upbringing and life experiences.

Have you ever been in a situation with your partner where you are feeling really connected and intimate, like she is the best woman you have ever been with? Then she says something that you interpret as critical and you immediately react by shutting down and pushing back in some way? You do not just think about your response; you get a full-body reaction. Parts of your body tense up and you feel a deep sense of abandonment or rejection—you embody that reaction. You have shape-shifted from *Lover* to *Abandoned* in a split-second. We are continually shape-shifting from archetype to archetype and their related personas from moment to moment.

Obviously if you spend your whole life shape-shifting from one positive, confident, happy, powerful archetype to another, you will have a happy and prosperous life. However, most of us develop negative embodiments of behavior that in some way limit our potential to be happy, prosperous and mentally and emotionally healthy at all times.

From my experience in life from the ages of 12 to 28, I fully embodied the beliefs that I wasn't worthy to be loved or happy. This came from internalized anger. I was a victim to my own belief that I was *a Sinner* because the religion I was raised in coerced me to believe that. It was hard for me to move out of those beliefs or shape-shift into another belief, because I didn't have the awareness or skill to do it.

At work in my mid-20's, I was the boss and I had to adopt the Leader/Manager archetype as best I could, but often from the place of being a Victim rather than a Victor. I would lead from a place of fear rather than of courage; consequently, my employees ran rings around me! I was constantly in survival mode.

We humans are malleable and easily influenced. What I learnt in my first experience with Amantane was that we have a choice in how to live our lives and what archetypal pattern we choose to express.

My choice, when He told me that *actions have consequences*, was to embark on my journey to my heart and soul, to explore how I could make more empowered, sovereign choices to be happy, to find love in my own heart—for myself. This has led to the greatest journey of my life, when I shape-shifted into the

Spiritual Seeker archetype, which I have been regularly embodying now for over 37 years.

EMBODIMENT STRATEGIES

Years ago, I did a shamanic journey to find a spirit guide who would help to elevate me at times of self-doubt. What was revealed to me felt like a past life. I was a South American warrior—bare chested. I was solo and paddling a dugout canoe. I was paddling with great strength and determination; I suddenly saw myself moving into a dense fog. The fog was so thick I couldn't see more than a few feet in any direction, but I kept going. The density of the fog didn't deter me one iota. I just knew where I had to paddle even though I had never been there before. Eventually the fog cleared and the vista opened up to a beautiful landscape, almost like a *Shambala* (spiritual kingdom). I paddled past a village where people were waving at me and were happy to see me because they were inspired by me for exiting the dense fog. The fog represented my mental challenges and doubts, but in moving through it, I found limitlessness, confidence and happiness. I became an inspiration to others. I use this image and shape-shift into the warrior whenever I feel like I can't do this work or when nagging self-doubt enters my thoughts. I embody my warrior, confident and determined—unwavering. In embodying him, I become him.

It's easy to change your behaviors and actions when you develop relationships to allies, real or imagined—like my warrior. You can *journey* to find an ally who can help you in a particular area of your life. Maybe the one ally can be enough, as in my case. I also work with different aspects of my healer self, but for my own personal emotional, psychological and spiritual self, I work with and embody my warrior.

By *journeying*, I mean just letting your imagination go off on its own with the intention of finding an ally. You know you are entering the subconscious realms, when the journey takes on a life of its own, rather than you directing it with conscious thought. You can use shamanic journeying music or shamanic drumming as an aid. There are many on the internet or on music apps. My favorite musician for both relaxing and journeying music is *Jonathan Goldman*.

If you are inspired by superheroes such as *Superman, Wonder Woman, Black Panther, Captain America, Thor*, etc., you can embody the strengths that they represent to you and notice how that feels. Get creative. Use any of these archetypal heroes to help you embody a different version of yourself. Maybe it's your dad or mum, or your grandfather or grandmother, or gods like *Isis* or *Hanuman*. Or maybe, like me, one just appears to you when you call them in.

Work with them regularly. I activate my guide whilst walking my dog, just to enhance and familiarize myself with him. He is ready any time I call him in. Am I creating him in my imagination or is he an alter ego? Is he a completely autonomous spirit ally? I don't know. I don't get bogged down in the details. I suggest you work with your spirit guides in the way that works best for you.

SOUL LOSS

Pain is the touchstone
Of all spiritual growth.

~ BILL W.

An important part of energy healing is the extraction of *Hucha* (Quechua term) or energetic density, otherwise known as energy intrusions.

These densities come into us as a result of trauma. When we have a traumatic experience, (usually in childhood), part of our spirit gets shocked out of our bodies leaving an energetic hole in us. This is known as *Soul Loss*. New energy that fills this hole, holds the signature of the original trauma or loss.

Memory loss can also occur at this point: this often reveals the age at which the soul loss occurred. If you cannot remember anything before age 7, for example, from the shamanic perspective, you have clearly suffered soul loss at age 7.

When something happens to remind us of the trauma surrounding our soul loss, the newly implanted energy starts to vibrate with the trauma memory and trigger's emotional reactions. We react as though the original event is happening. PTSD conditions, panic attacks, and feelings of abandonment or danger, are some examples of reactions that occur. *To permanently change feelings that are being triggered, the energy density needs to be extracted.*

These dense energies can contain the thought forms of people of influence, such as parents or teachers. They cause us to act out from that influence, as though their voices are in our heads, causing us to react in anger, fear, doubt, etc. Maybe they carry our father's anger, or our mother's sense of self-doubt? These also contain ancestral woundings and are aptly named *baggage*—we are literally carrying them around as though we have the weight of the world on our shoulders.

These thought forms are so deeply embedded within us, they feel like us—but they are not. Without these *dense balls of energy* in our bodies, we would be free of the energetic influence that they contain.

HEALING THE WHOLE BODY

When someone comes to me for a healing session, I usually have no idea of their conditions beforehand. They may have anxiety, depression, sexual trauma, cancer, or deep fears that are keeping them stuck in a chronic condition. They may keep sabotaging relationships, or have deep anger issues.

So how can I help shift so many different issues without pills or whirly gigs? I have a strategy!

I start by finding out why they are living in a fear-based state. Pretty much everyone who comes to me does, even if they don't identify it as that. It tends to be our *go to* state. You can be 6′ 6″ and 280 lbs. of solid muscle, a tough macho man, and still hold fear in your body. Size and physical strength do not matter. I have seen many a *tough guy* reduced to a whimpering mess in an Ayahuasca Ceremony.

I am looking for high impact events in their lives that may have caused the conditions they are suffering from. I am examining events which caused their original soul and subsequent power loss. This helps them to understand why they have been reacting in self-limiting ways. Most of my clients come without any previous knowledge of soul loss.

I then help my clients access deep feelings and emotions through my fusion of methods. Once I have led them to the sweet spot, I am able to *see* where the block occurred to allow me to extract it. Once the dense energy is removed and replaced with a vibrant energy (I use Reiki for this), they can start to re-imagine a better life. The body and soul know what to do at this point to allow for optimum healing.

If I feel they are ready, I will then do the Shamanic process known as *soul retrieval*—to bring back the lost soul fragments. This process is not covered in this book, as it is extensive, but is offered as part of my Shamanistic Reiki trainings.

When the client moves back into a harmonious state, not only do the symptoms go away but the causes of the symptoms are released. The more fully they release, the more fully they heal, whatever the condition.

Because traditional talk therapy does not include processes of energy extraction or soul retrieval, the root cause of a person's dis-ease may never fully heal. Therefore, a full transformation of beliefs, behaviors and reactions is unlikely to occur.

MY SUPER POWER

There is a superhero in all of us,
We just need the courage to put on the cape.

~ SUPERMAN

I have received many teachings from Grandmother Ayahuasca on how to best serve others. That included learning how to *see* where the blocks are and how to remove them to get the energy flowing again. This is what I experienced when Maestro Pedro sucked *hucha* from my damaged ear to help heal my tinnitus in my first Ayahuasca ceremony.

After five or six years of working with the medicine in ceremony, She told me: **"Okay, you're ready to suck now!"** I hadn't tried it before, or even thought about doing so, and then suddenly I could just do it! She showed me in that instant, something that I wasn't even aware that I was quietly training for.

This extraction process which Ayahuasca taught me is *my superpower*—the one that has the most dramatic impact on my clients' mental, emotional and physical well-being. Following this process, I typically ask my clients how they are feeling. They usually answer: "I feel light" or "I feel lighter". The magic words!

You only recognize how heavy something is, when it is no longer there; it's as though you've had a heavy backpack removed from your shoulders. The lightness that ensues, allows you to act in a light way. With feelings of lightness, you start to react with expressions of positivity and happiness.

There is no way to really know how the removal of these dense energies will unfold in your life, but you will likely be happier, healthier and more loving to yourself.

Susan's Story

Susan came to my office complaining of her persistent need to sabotage her relationships. She had an intellectual understanding of why she kept doing it but didn't seem to be able to change her behaviors. I questioned her about her early life and found out **she had been put straight into an incubator at birth; this usually manifests as a fear of abandonment and not feeling worthy to be loved.** We tend to play out our inner belief systems and this was why she kept repeating the same old behaviors. I performed an energy extraction on the significant density I saw in her root chakra, which is associated with feelings of abandonment and lack of safety. I also removed density from her sacral chakra, which is associated with relationships. Afterward, she expressed how much lighter she felt as a result of the extractions.

In a follow up session, Susan said how much more positive she felt with herself (relationship with self being our primary relationship) and that her chronic lower back pain had completely gone away. She had not told me about the back pain before. Lower back pain is related to the sacral chakra that affects sexuality and relationships.

DENSITY RELEASING EXERCISE

Have you developed an awareness of what your density triggers are and how they restrict your behaviors and belief systems? How could this be influencing your overall well-being? Make a list and locate where you feel them in your body—even if you feel like you're making it up. Can you trace the originating source of each one through . . . :

- *Feeling*
- *Observing*
- *Remembering*

Stay with the sensations for a while and see how the memories or influence held in each energy ball has affected you and notice if you can sense where it originally came from.

With a quartz crystal, rub the areas where you hold the individual densities and one at a time give them to the crystal. Say "I let you go, I set you free" for each one. Breathe a cleansing breath or two into each area as you do the release.

There is an integration period after the energy release that takes a few weeks. During that period, you may feel dense emotions rising to the surface as they move out of your body: anger, fear, self-doubt, melancholy, etc., that seem to come out of nowhere. Recognize that the emotions are releasing from deep within you. Let them go—set them free. Use your hands or a feather to brush them off, rather than internalize them as you may have done in the past. Smudge yourself with white sage (burn dried white sage and pass the smoke over your body).

Say out loud "I let you go. I set you free", as you brush them away with a theatrical wave of the hand or a feather fan. You will feel lighter.

FUCK THAT SHIT

The last of the human freedoms—
To choose one's attitude in any given situation.
~ VICTOR FRANKL

I use the above expression (FTS) as a way to release unwanted behaviors and beliefs in my own and my clients conditioned responses. We develop belief systems that hold a lower vibration than what we prefer to carry around with us. Is it real or is it just something that we have allowed to inhabit our psychological, emotional and energetic space? I have found that the FTS expression, sounds both humorous and cavalier and it can allow for an almost comic relationship to issues that we have had a futile relationship with in the past. To make light of the heaviness can bring a release of the tension we hold in our bodies around it.

Depression: Fuck that shit!

Fear of heights: Fuck that shit!

Trauma around sexual abuse: Fuck that shit!

All the negative thoughts that I keep replaying in my mind: Fuck that shit!

Saying it with a cocky tone and laughing at the ridiculousness of it all, can help you let go of negative old stories. I encourage clients to use this phrase while brushing off density from any area of their body where they feel the hucha is held—while saying *Fuck that Shit!*

Making light of an issue as it reoccurs can loosen the hold it has over you. Stoicism is a good way to solve problems in the mind whereas, humor is a good way to solve problems in the body and with emotions. As you say *Fuck that Shit* and brush away the problem, notice how it feels to do that. Do you feel lighter? Be encouraged by any noticeable shift.

This is not to diminish the impact that a trauma has had on you, but it's also good to see the light-hearted side of how you keep reliving and defining the future, because you keep responding in the same way to the past.

It may seem odd initially to laugh at your sexual abuse or feelings of worthlessness, but you've got to start somewhere. Why not just try, *Fuck that Shit!* Taking it less seriously is worth a try. Let the density go, bit by bit. Open yourself up to a new possibility. What have you got to lose?

I questioned myself as to why I wanted to keep being depressed. Because I didn't want to lose the fifteen years of already being depressed? Really? Amantane said, **"Who cares— only you."** I recognized instantly the funny side of that and felt an immediate release inside. It was a turning point for me. To see the humor in my limiting beliefs, I was able to move forward in making changes because I was no longer completely trapped within them. Fuck that shit!

I have helped many clients see how the serious relationship they have with their affliction has contributed to their staying in darkness. After guiding them through a laughter release, they often say the magic words, "I feel a lot lighter!"

F.T.S. EXERCISE

Write a list of your five biggest drawbacks or limitations in life, that you feel keep you tethered to neurotic dependency. Close your eyes and try to see the funny side of why you continue to react in a particular way. Say "Fuck that Shit"—as you brush each one away to help lighten the load. "I let you go. I set you free."

I sometimes say that the human experience is God's reality TV show.

Imagine that you are seeing yourself as an observer, as though you were watching yourself in a reality TV show and acting out like one of the neurotic participants. Try seeing the humor in it and laugh at yourself. You will notice a release.

Jenny's Story

Jenny came to me because she was completely stuck in her life. She didn't know what she wanted to do in her career, where she wanted to live or whether she should go back to school. She was only 36, but she couldn't see a bright future for herself. Additionally, she hadn't been in a relationship for 10 years. We had quite a light-hearted session with a lot of laughter and I helped her to see her condition in a more humorous way without diminishing the seriousness of her personal challenges.

Also, as part of the session I helped her to see where some of her beliefs were held in her body and how that led to her self-doubt. I then did my Shamanic Energy Extraction. She expressed how she felt lighter and with that came more hopefulness for her future. She left with a skip in her step.

She emailed me two days after the session. She wrote that she had met a guy on the train going home from our session and that she was going out on a date with him! Jenny ended up marrying that guy. She also got a new job that she loved. That is the power of energy flow, through both laughter and energy extraction!

28

PILLOW TALK TO FEEL SAFE

Wherever your heart is,
Your mind will be also.

~ PARAMAHANSA YOGANANDA

A pillow can help you to connect with the place inside of you that feels safe, soft and comfortable, where safety resides. Safety is there and always has been there. Now we are going to access this place and feel what safety represents to you.

Some words that describe feeling safe are: relaxed, secure, warm, comfortable, peaceful, restful, happy, and calm. You cannot feel safe unless you feel what these words represent.

PILLOW EXERCISE

Sit with a pillow on your lap as a prop and close your eyes. Put your hands flat on the pillow and lengthen your inhale and exhale. Notice how it feels to expand your breath. Tune into the feelings in your hands, wrists and forearms supported by the pillow. Do a few rounds of deep breathing to notice the effects that deep breathing has on your body and mental state.

Squeeze the pillow and notice how it feels. Notice how the pillow adds an extra layer of support for your hands and wrists. Notice your feelings in relationship to the pillow. Soften and surrender to those feelings. How can you soften more into the feelings of surrender? Take those feelings deeper.

Take your time and allow your body to get familiar with the feelings . . .

Notice how soft, comfortable, safe and supportive the pillow feels . . .

Keeping your eyes closed. Spend five or more minutes enjoying this. Squeeze the pillow if it helps.

Next, notice that the feelings you have relating to the pillow are not the pillow's feelings, they are yours. Isn't it amazing how quickly you were able to access feelings of safety? These feelings of safety are NOT from outside of yourself—they co-exist with all of your feelings.

This simple process helps you access the foundational feeling of safety which is required for your transformation.

You cannot change your life if you do not feel safe to do so.

Say "Thank you, body (or say your name) for allowing me to experience these beautiful, gentle feelings. It feels safe. I feel safe."

Spend some time with your feelings associated with the pillow. Enjoy it. Remember the feelings of safety have always been there and have always been accessible. It is only your hypervigilant self that has prevented you from connecting to that safe place within you.

Now when you are ready you can open your eyes and come back into the room.

Isn't this encouraging? Does it make you want to access this place more often? What if you accessed this place a few times a day? Your body and your subconscious would then be able to access this place more easily. It would become the new norm. Accessing this place is the antidote to fear and tension. Familiarize yourself with this place. It's safe, its peaceful, its gentle. Do it for yourself. Nobody else can do it for you.

Imagine if you had learnt to access this place when you were young and afraid. But when you were young, you were dependent on others for your safety. Now you're not. Now you can rely on yourself for your own safety. And you have it right here.

It has always been here and it always is here. All you have to do is let go of the tension and feel it. Notice how it feels to feel safe.

Every experience in life has feelings associated with it. Allow feelings. Recognize you have full autonomy, full control over what feelings you want to be dominant.

Isn't it amazing that just by allowing soft feelings, initially with the help of the soft pillow, you have full control over the feelings you experience in this moment. It's remarkable how you can access a place of safety so easily after years of hypervigilance and fear. This is the path of self-mastery.

This path to healing can seem too simple, but that is the beauty of it. You can laugh at how simple it is and why your resistance or unawareness of how to surrender has caused hardship and negativity. It can also be exciting to recognize that you have so much control over how your body and mind reacts.

Sara's Story

Sara, a client in her 50's, came to me with deep trauma. The description of her trauma at the hands of her ex-husband was probably the worst I had ever heard. Her story made my blood boil, though I didn't show it. I'm not disclosing the details because of the severity of her experience.

How can I help you? I asked

"I want to experience vulnerability" she said. "I am afraid to be vulnerable because I am afraid of my emotions, my feelings."

With the aid of Reiki, breathwork and guided imagery, she soon entered a very relaxed state. I took her into her feelings. With her eyes closed, she was smiling. *How does that feel Sara?* "Oh my God, it feels amazing" she responded. *Do you know what that is Sara?* I asked. *That's vulnerability! How do you feel about vulnerability now?*

"It's beautiful. It's not scary at all. And it's so simple!"

When she was ready energetically and emotionally, I did my Shamanic Energy Extraction.

I bumped into Sara about a year later. She told me her life had completely changed following our two sessions. She was happier, more confident and above all she allowed herself to really feel her feelings and to love herself in a deeper way than she ever had. Her 20 yr. old daughter who was with her, beamed at me as Sara spoke to me enthusiastically.

Jon's Story

I had a Japanese client, Jon, who came to me because he said he could not feel his feelings. He was guarded and had not been able to express his feelings in his family, which is very common in Asian families. Using the pillow exercise, I guided him out of his head and through his resistance. Quickly he was able to describe his experience (with one-word answers).

I asked him: *Who's feelings are those?*

"They are mine!" he responded.

Then you are accessing your feelings.

He laughed and said, "Oh my God, that's so simple, isn't it?"

He trusted himself to go deeper. After a lifetime of denying that he could access his feelings, he realized in that moment that he had disassociated his body experiences from his mind. Just to bring him into his body and point out that his experiences were his own felt experiences, changed his relationship to his feelings. He realized there was nothing to be afraid of.

I allow my clients to explore expanded states which they describe as incredible, safe, amazing, peaceful, happy, light, gentle, fantastic. I help them to have a gentle journey into these states and to recognize that they have full autonomy to enter those uplifting states any time they choose. They become aware that they also have full responsibility over experiencing dense, negative states. It is their choice to contract or expand. It is a simple journey, an easy one. Clients often report that they haven't felt this good in years.

Whatever good feelings my clients describe, I remind them that this is the feeling of healing. They have gently guided their bodies to enter into the state where healing occurs. The full extent of what that shift creates will unfold over the coming months.

BODY LOVE

When you make the decision physically to do something,
Also make the decision mentally
So, you're not working against yourself.

~ MAXWELL MALTZ

How many times have you looked in a mirror and wished that another version of yourself were looking back at you? How many times have you wished you were taller or shorter, fatter or thinner, blond or brunette or had different teeth or jawline?

How often do you take your mental, emotional and physical well-being for granted until it is taken away? I encourage you to honor your body in a deeper way. Show deep gratitude for everything your body gives you rather than what it doesn't. We are not all Olympic athletes or Runway models. We come in many shapes, sizes and flavors. Many people want to change something about themselves that they don't feel good about, even though nobody else notices. The best way to live is to feel good about yourself even if you are not the idealized version that has been programmed into you by the media or peer pressure—which changes depending on the current trend.

In his classic book *Psycho-Cybernetics*, Dr. Maxwell Maltz, considered the grandfather of self-help, wrote about clients who never seemed to be happy with themselves. A successful plastic surgeon, Dr. Maltz recognized that he was often wasting his time and his patient's money by doing plastic surgery to change a nose or a breast size, when the problem was a perception in the mind of his client. No matter what he did to create a more idealized nose or breast, the client still wasn't happy, even though Dr. Maltz thought the surgery or the original version was fine. It became clear to Dr. Maltz that his time would be better spent and his clients would be better served, if he helped to change their minds rather than their bodies. He spent a lifetime having great success in his workshops helping to change lives by changing the minds of tens of thousands of people.

It's time to honor all aspects of your body. Your body is a sensitive conscious organism and responds to both criticism and praise. When you hold negative beliefs about your body, your body responds with feelings of shame. If you believe your body is less than you desire, it will give you a lesser version of itself in both health and wellbeing. Autoimmune conditions can often be linked to your body rejecting itself because you have rejected your body. You create your own physical reality through your thoughts.

HOW TO HONOR YOUR BODY EXERCISE

I frequently thank my physical body for keeping me healthy, strong and vibrant. My body consequently heals very quickly if injured or sick. I regularly speak to my body and I recommend you try it using your own words.

"Thank you, Body, I am so grateful for everything you have done for me throughout my life. How you keep me healthy, despite all the many ways I abused you when I was younger—with drugs, alcohol, tobacco and unhealthy foods—you keep coming back to a state of good health. It's miraculous how you recover and are pain free. Thank you for stepping up for me and allowing me to live in a pain-free, healthy way. Thank you, dear Lungs, for breathing. Even if there are toxins in the environment or smoke in the air caused by forest fires, you keep breathing and recover quickly. Dear Heart, thank you for beating so strongly and pumping the oxygen around my body in my blood to feed all of me. Thank you, Arms, for being strong and flexible. Thank you, Hands, for being dexterous and allowing me to have earned a living for so many years and for responding so quickly to my desires. I am so grateful. It's good to touch you, to inhabit your physical form, to feel a connection. I love you so much."

Use your sense of touch to notice how your body responds. Connect with yourself in a much more mindful way.

"Thank you, Body, I am so grateful for all of you."

Start at the top of your head and continue down your body to your feet.

If you feel resistance in any area, relax and pay extra attention until you feel a softening and deeper sense of gratitude.

An additional powerful way to do this is to stand naked in front of a mirror as you do the exercises.

To be in gratitude to your body is a beautiful process of self-honoring. Get massages, Reiki or other types of energy healing sessions. Give your body clean water, good food, fresh air. Pamper yourself in body-honoring activities, so that it can feel restored. Meditate and engage in pursuits that relieve stress. Breathe mind-fully. Any activity that supports your body's well-being will give you a richer, healthier life.

Julia's Story

Julia, the most physically beautiful woman with whom I have ever worked, came to me because she had deep anxiety about her looks and could only see her perceived flaws. With the anxiety this caused her, she could barely breathe. It was not my place to negate her experience of herself and insist on her how beautiful she was; what I could do was to get to the root cause of why she saw such a diminished version of herself.

It turned out that the root cause of her issue was that her father never gave her validation or showed her that he loved her. She was also sexually abused by a relative, which turned her against her own beauty, as she saw it subconsciously as a liability and made her feel dirty. Her subconscious mind only allowed her eyes to see "ugly" and "unlovable" when she looked in the mirror.

In her session, I focused on helping her to feel safe and lovable, and I also helped to release the energetic trauma of her youth by doing my Shamanic Energy Extraction. Soon after, she reported "at last I can breathe freely, for the first time in my life." That healing allowed her to release the anxiety-based tension she held in her body and she soon started to feel better about herself.

30

"I LOVE YOU"

Love is the first law of life.

~ JESUS

These are the three most powerful words in the English language—especially when spoken to yourself.

FEELING THE LOVE EXERCISE

Close your eyes and put one or both hands on your heart. Take a few breaths. Relax. Say to yourself out loud, "I Love You." Remember, you are saying this 100% to yourself. Now say it again but this time say it with a deeper commitment. "I Love You." Say it again and again, and each time see if you can surrender and open not just to the words but to the vibration of the words. "I LOVE YOU." Say your name, "_____, I Love You." See if you can say it so it evokes a tear or two. "_____, I Love You." Let the vibration of the words flow to every cell of your body. Feel the words "I Love You" all the way to the tips of your fingers and toes. Bask in the glow of the self-love. See if you can absorb it in a deeper way than you have ever felt it before. The experience of love is a sensation. Breathe it in. Learn how simple it is to feel love by simply surrendering and allowing that feeling to happen. If you can't feel it, then you are resisting it. It's there. Open and expand yourself.

If English is your second language, say the equivalent of "I Love You" in your native tongue, as it has more meaning and is more powerful.

If you still feel resistance to this practice, try over-emphasizing your expression of love to yourself. In other words, ham it up. Over act. Your subconscious doesn't know you are being theatrical. It is taking it all in and will respond appropriately.

It's a good way to get through the block. As always, notice how it feels and be encouraged with any small shift in sensations towards your heart opening. Have fun with it. Don't be so serious about loving yourself. It's **not** loving yourself that is serious.

This is something that I learnt to do to help myself not be depressed, to make better choices—to decide to live an exceptional life—to write this book!

Peter's Story

Peter was a client whom I tried to coax into "Feeling the Love" as described above. He initially refused to do it because he felt awkward, exposed and resistant. I gently suggested: *Would you be willing to give it a try? After all, you came here for something?* and I showed him how to do it.

Very stiffly he said "I Love You." It sounded quite forced and 1 out of 10 for commitment. With some gentle encouragement, he quickly got it up to about a 6 out of 10. At that point he started crying. I asked him how he felt. He replied "It feels nice!" It's that simple. In that moment he experienced alchemy, as he turned lead into gold.

Peter accessed a place of vulnerability and willingness to feel love. He had protected his heart his whole life because he felt it kept him safe from the emotional pain he had experienced as a child. It was beautiful to witness the softening and to know that this simple experience would help to change his life.

When Peter said, "It feels nice," I decided not to interrupt his experience by suggesting that he change the wording to "I feel nice." I didn't want him to lose the moment. But saying "I feel nice" or "I feel" anything, is more powerful. "IT" is still keeping some distance from a personalized experience, but in this case, it was a victory and progress for Peter.

With your heart opening to stimulate a sense of well-being, you naturally and easily feel surrounded by love, compassion and happiness with a deep connection to your inner world. What once seemed challenging can now flow with ease and grace and you can be filled with expansive connection to your Divine self and a state of love.

MIRROR WORK EXERCISE

With a hand-held mirror (use one that frames your face), take a long look at your face. Look into your eyes. Be vulnerable. See yourself. Recognize your beauty. What does it feel like to make a commitment to the you who is looking back at you? You are not looking for flaws; you are there to access the beauty, to see yourself in a new way. This is not the time for negative self-talk, just self-approval. After all, if you don't approve of yourself, you can't move into loving yourself.

This process is about feeling into it, not thinking into it. Disregard self-sabotaging thoughts like, "What If I'm not doing it right?" Do the best you can and then do better!

    Say to yourself as you look into your own eyes:

    "What can I do to love you more?"

    "How can you feel more seen?"

    "What do you need to feel more heard?"

    "How can I see you with more honesty?"

    "I make a commitment to you to feel happier."

    "I Love You So Much."

    Spend time just looking at yourself. Surrender to yourself. What is required to feel approval, kindness and affection from yourself? What can you do to heal any criticisms or disapproval of yourself? This is the deepest work you can do.

    Do this process slowly. Feel each uplifting thing you express to yourself. Keep a relaxed gaze. Breathe deeply. Notice any resistance and simply soften through it. Are you willing to allow tears?

    Recognize in these softer moments with yourself how every positive experience feels good, and any tension pulls you away from that feeling of positivity or self-approval. Play with it: explore it.

If you develop a deeper connection to yourself by becoming more aware of yourself and loving you, why would you act out with repeated behaviors that aren't for your highest good?

    If you notice any resistance still, see if you can explore what the resistance represents. Sometimes it is just a feeling of awkwardness over reaching a new level of intimacy with yourself.

Intimacy = In to Me I See

    Your heart doesn't need protecting. The reality is it can take care of itself. Let it now take care of you. Live fully from a place of love. It's your mind that is disconnecting you from the infinite wisdom and unlimited potential that has always been there. Speak and engage with this process in the most fully embodied way that you can and keep deepening. At some point it becomes the most natural thing in the world and as a result your world will change.

31

RAISING THE VIBRATION TO EMPTY MIND

Many clients have come to me over the years who have had long term insomnia, which is generally related to disruptive thoughts because of a stressful job or home life. They may have a history of anxiety that often stems from early onset hypervigilance, the causes of which are many, but generally lead back to having been raised in an environment that felt unsafe.

I use a process that helps to raise the energetic vibration of the client, and in so doing it helps with relaxation and emptying the mind. This technique can be so successful that negative or disruptive thoughts can't even enter your conscious awareness, even if you try to make that happen. Clients often laugh at the moment they experience an empty mind for the first time, as they realize how easy it is to do.

EMPTY MIND EXERCISE

Use a pillow on your lap as in Chapter 28 to enhance this exercise. First, close your eyes and breathe in a relaxed way. Spend a few minutes breathing deeply into your diaphragm. Extend and expand your breath so you bring in more oxygen and release more fully on the exhale. Notice how with your lengthened breath, your body just naturally relaxes. On the inhale, recognize what a vital life-force your breath is. Enjoy breathing more fully.

As you notice yourself relaxing, observe how amazing this feels and how quickly you are able to release tension.

After a few minutes of this, start to make a sound on the exhale. With your mouth open, make a guttural sound that is the hum of the Earth's resonance. Explore this a bit until you feel you have hit this note. Notice the sound go to the tips of your toes on the exhale. Then when you have done this, imagine that the sound is going to every cell of your body on its way out of your toes. Expand your awareness in the best way you can while doing this.

Say out loud "I feel relaxed." Go deeper into the feeling of relaxed. Notice how you can open and soften even more.

Say things like:
"I feel great."
"I feel incredible."
"I feel safe."
"I feel happy."
"I feel calm."
"I feel good."
"I feel peaceful."
"I feel amazing."

Imagine that your voice speaking these words out loud is sound healing for the soul. *As you say these sentences, exaggerate your voice so you are emphatic about what these words mean to you. Notice the subtle differences within each word. Feel the words you speak.*

When you feel these feelings and are comfortable with feeling them—go deeper!

You will find that very quickly you feel yourself in an elevated vibratory state. When you are in this state, lower vibratory experiences can't inhabit this space. Your mind will be empty of the self-limiting chatter.

Spend as long as you want in this space and explore ways to go deeper into the peaceful and expansive feelings. You are working in the subtle realms where magic happens and you enter the Unified Field.

THE UNIFIED FIELD

In this expanded state, you are entering the unified field of consciousness, where you experience universal wisdom outside of your body. This is the field of information that governs all the laws of nature. You feel whole; you are whole. In this state, you receive wisdom and knowledge and are also in the state where deep mental and emotional healing occur. This can influence physical imbalances in the body and allow for physical healing. Energy flows: love flows: you feel at peace: there is no stress. Ayahuasca can take you there and so can your unique mind.

Once you have experienced it, you want more of it, for this is life on the other side of resistance. Open. Expanded. Free! In this state you want the best for yourself; you want the best for everyone. This is the bliss state written about by the mystical poets. It is always there, within your grasp. You do not need psychedelics to access it, though sometimes they can be an asset to help show you how to get there. You do not need to depend on them; in fact, learn not to depend on them to access this expanded state.

Expanded consciousness is everywhere—outside of time and space, where all knowledge already exists. It is here, it is now, it is everywhere and it is nowhere. There is no separation, no You or I. The brain and body are receptors that receive waves of electromagnetism containing everything. It is all accessible to you: memories, awareness, knowledge, love. All thoughts already exist. Everything is contained within these fields. You experience God: You Are Creation.

BREATH

Every breath is a prayer.
Every breath is a blessing.

~ DAN BRULÉ

You breathe in the manner in which you live and you live in the manner in which you breathe. If you breathe fully, you live fully.

It is well known amongst breath workers that specific emotions are associated with specific breathing patterns. If you breathe short erratic, tense breaths, you live in an erratic, tense state. If you breathe in a relaxed, conscious and aware way, you live in a relaxed, conscious and aware way. If you breathe slowly and deliberately, your experience is more deliberate, more expansive—calmer. The additional oxygen allows you to live a healthier and more power-filled life.

To breathe powerfully is to live powerfully.

Breath contains love. Breathing more fully brings more love into your body. Is that not an easy path to health and happiness?

Conscious breathing helps to activate the subconscious mind and bring awareness and insights not easily accessed through traditional therapy. Breath opens the energy channels in the body and neural pathways in the brain. This allows for what we have been holding onto, to surface and be released.

I have had insights and visionary experiences with conscious breathwork, similar to an Ayahuasca journey—so have many of my clients. During our Ayahuasca retreats, on non-drinking days, I sometimes guide participants in breathwork sessions. They have often reported being *back in the medicine* and gaining clarity over experiences they had in ceremony. Recently a client on retreat had a very powerful *father wound* healing during her breathwork session, which had not been healed during any of her many previous Ayahuasca ceremonies.

This is the reason I use multiple healing modalities, as one never knows which one will offer the deepest healing and subsequently yield the greatest transformation.

Most of us don't breathe fully. When we learn to breathe fully and consciously, we are able to liberate what we have been resisting and thus open ourselves to an incredible expansion of self-awareness and self-love. If you're willing to breathe more consciously you're willing to feel your feelings. If you wish to learn more about true breath mastery, I highly recommend Dan Brulé's book, *Just Breathe*.

Your first inhale when your umbilical cord was cut was your first purely autonomous act in this life, separate from your mother. Your last autonomous act in this life, will be your last exhale. What you do with each of your hundreds of millions of autonomous breaths in between, is within your power to decide.

When I teach my breathwork trainings, I include shamanic techniques that enhance the healing potential of the sessions. I call my training *Freedom Breathwork*. It incorporates a slow breathing style coupled with guided imagery and insightful inquiry. I have found this to be a powerful tool for Ayahuasca integration.

Freedom Breathwork incorporates a technique known as conscious, connected breath. Breathing in and breathing out with no gaps between the inhale and the exhale. It is also a circular breath. As with the rest of my teachings, I am all about the simple path. This is one of the simplest yet transformative breathing techniques.

CONNECTED BREATHWORK EXERCISE

Imagine it like the waves on the shore. As one wave rolls in, there is another wave just waiting to roll in after the previous wave has rolled out, in a beautiful synchronized flow of energy.

Receive with the active inhale.

Let go with the passive exhale.

As you inhale, invoke to yourself—"I receive."

As you exhale, invoke to yourself—"I release."

You can then add what it is you wish to receive and what you want to release.

Oxygen contains Love, along with life force.

As you inhale, invoke "I breathe in Love."

As you exhale, invoke "I breathe out Love."

After ten minutes of using your breath to calm and center you, you may notice other internal shifts, as you move into the sweet spot of breathing.

Now use your breath to expand your consciousness. Imagine with each inhale, with the increased oxygen flow, you are expanding your conscious awareness so that it grows and magnifies beyond your physical form, surrounding you in a cocoon of love.

To eventually set yourself free in a bubble of celestial light, floating in the limitlessness of your Sacredness.

METAMORPHOSIS

After all, what is a butterfly if not the flowering of a caterpillar
beyond its wildest dreams?

Emerging from the womb of the chrysalis, the butterfly
discards its restrictive silken shell, to inherit a magical new
world of flowers, breezes and sunshine.

A world of freedom and delight and a celebration
of its divine nature.

Spreading her wings for the first time, she has
no idea whether she can fly.

She simply opens her wings in perfect confidence and is
effortlessly conveyed into the spiral dance of graceful flight.

And all that then remains is the joyous participation
in the divine ecstasy of creation.

~ FROM THE POEM BY DARPAN

Breathe That In . . .

EPILOGUE

The secret to life is,
That it ends.

~ FRANZ KAFKA

Everything I wrote about here is common sense. You know it all already. Your mind and body know it all already. Happiness, peace, love, abundance and health are all here already. They co-exist with fear, anger, lack, disease, and sickness. Which do you want as the dominant force in your life?

I have recounted a few experiences of my life and travels thus far. What I am trying to illustrate, is that this journey of life is a university of learning and we all leave life with a doctorate in knowledge. Whether that develops into a doctorate in wisdom depends on how much awareness we develop.

We are human and as humans we all have issues, blind spots and problems to deal with. Some are existential problems, some financial or relational. We have our own ways of dealing with them the best we can. All the circumstances of our lives are opportunities to build wisdom and learn how to be better and wiser versions of ourselves.

My singing teacher once told me that if I wanted to learn to sing at a higher pitch, I had to first learn to sing to a lower pitch. To stretch my voice higher meant learning to sing lower and lower. *The lower I could sink meant the higher I could rise.* I see this teaching as a metaphor for life. See the depths that you may have sunken into as an opportunity now to elevate your-

207

self to ever higher heights of happiness. Imagine the power this could generate—to ultimately claim *your superpower!*

My journey from depression in my 20's to a life of abundant happiness has been an incredible path of learning. Every single moment has had value. My character, my personality, the wisdom gained—heavily influenced by my beloved spiritual teachers, Ayahuasca and Amantane, is the cumulative result of a countless number of small actions, beliefs and thoughts—from moment, to moment, to moment. Nothing has been wasted. Every purge into a bucket, every tear shed, has been a peeling back of the layers of resistance to move deeper into self-awareness, into deeper self-love.

Without Ayahuasca I would not actively be living the life I have since the mid-2000's. Now I live in Ecuador, where I am working closely with the indigenous healers of this magical land. I owe a huge debt of gratitude to the sacred plants and human teachers for giving me so much and showing me how to live my best life.

We are all at different stages of spiritual development and awareness and we can only operate from the level of the awareness that we have.

My hope for us all is that we keep learning from our experiences and stop repeating restrictive reactions and behaviors. Even if you don't consider yourself a spiritual seeker, you want to be happy and free of suffering. When you say "Yes" to living life fully, as I did, you make the choice to operate from a place of greater understanding and fulfillment—from a higher vibratory state of lightness.

When Amantane told me to go find an Indian village and spend three months there to recreate my life and build my character—the time period was significant. This could not have been done in a month. In the same way, I encourage you to spend 90 days doing the exercises in Part III daily, to entrain your subconscious to reconnect with your Divine Truth—I make clear choices—I am safe—I am worthy to be loved—I am love.

When I discovered this teaching by His Holiness the XIV Dalai Lama while traveling in Nepal in the 1980's (I first saw it on a T-shirt), I was inspired to use it as a mantra for the way I wish to live my life and do my work. I continue to use it as a point of reference for myself and share it with my clients to also inspire them.

No matter what is going on—Never give up
Develop the heart
Too much energy in your country is spent developing the mind
Instead of the heart
Be compassionate
Not just to your friends—But to everyone
Be compassionate
Work for peace—In your heart and in the world
Work for peace
And I say again—Never give up
No matter what is going on around you—Never give up.

Remember my friends:
Life doesn't have to be that hard.
Walk in Beauty.
Never Give Up!
Be Extraordinary.

With a deep bow of respect to all our teachers: seen and unseen. To the wisdoms that you have so kindly imparted to us. Sharing your homes, your traditions, your medicine ways, your food, your support, your friendship and your love. Thank you from the depths of our hearts. We promise to always honor you and to share your wisdom and kindness with others, that they may also share it, till the thread of connectivity and compassion reaches out in a gentle wave of healing resonance to encircle the whole of Pachamama for the collective healing of all: United in One Heart—One Breath.

Much Love,
Alan and Dianna
Mt. Shasta, California and
Vilcabamba, Ecuador 2023

P.S. We would love to hear from you about your significant life changes.

APPENDIX

What is Shamanism?

I have used the word Shaman or Shamanism throughout this book and want to describe core premises about what that means, as it seems to be largely misunderstood and misused.

Shamanism is a complicated thing to explain, as there is no one empirical wisdom to describe exactly what it is, with each culture where it is practiced giving a different version of what it means. Even within that context it is constantly re-shaped and re-framed and as such, it could be considered a *spiritual technology* dependent on the current needs of the community or tribe. It is a way of life, a spiritual path and a source of income.

Shamanism is a wisdom tradition that has been practiced in its many forms for at least 40,000 years under the premise that if it works, use it and if it doesn't, don't bother. This is a good axiom and the reason it has been practiced for hundreds of generations.

Some in the West may think of it as folk or holistic healing, possibly incorporating herbalism, witchcraft, psychology, holistic doctoring, mediumship, spiritual mentoring, etc. Shamanism has at its core, a practitioner called a Shaman whose job it is to take care of the spiritual and health needs of the tribe or community where they work and as such, they tend to be the Leader or Oracle of the community. Shamanism in indigenous cultures is mostly an oral tradition and teachings are usually observed by an apprentice rather than directly taught by the Shaman. It is considered a job and is the way that people trained as Shamans support their family.

Shamanism stems from the belief that we live in an animistic reality. The root of Animism is the Greek word *Anima* which means: Breath, Life, Spirit. The web of life is an animated one and is alive. All phenomena have consciousness and spirit and can be communicated with. The trees, the water, the rocks, the stars, trains, planes and automobiles are all alive. If one thing is out of balance, everything is out of balance. Animism teaches right relationship with nature to bring it back to balance.

Right relationship with nature is right relationship with self.

Although western scholars can only pontificate over what a Shaman actually is, there is a common agreement over the core attributes that the Shaman possesses:

- Believes in the existence of the Spirit world which has direct influence on the physical world.
- Can enter a trance state to connect with elements of the spirit world to bring back healing energies, direct revelation and wisdom for the benefit of the community.
- Can access trance states through plant medicine journeys, though it's more common for the Shaman to access the non-ordinary states necessary to do their work, through ecstatic drumming, singing and dancing.
- Can *at-will* enter these non-ordinary states of reality within the imaginal realms, to engage with spirit helpers, ancestors, angels, ascended masters, and forces of nature to develop relationships, solve problems, perform healings and enhance balance.

The shamanic view is that the weakened soul or spirit is the cause of sickness, weakness or imbalance of the physical, emotional or mental body. This is usually the result of trauma, soul-loss, or a compromised energy field.

Shamanism in the West has developed a meaning of its own. In recent years it has become a popular internet search word and has become very romanticized. I hear it used in very general terms to describe yoga teachers, hair-dressers, artists and breathwork practitioners, amongst many other things. The significance of the word is different to someone using it in the party scene in Los Angeles than to a member of the Tungus Tribe in Siberia, where it originated. It is a power word and even though misused, it has developed a life of its own that can help the user develop trust and confidence in the person whom they are describing as *shaman*. For that reason—

if it works, use it—if it doesn't, don't bother!

TRAININGS

You may arrive a victim,
But you won't leave as one.

~ A.F.W.

At the time of this writing, 2023, I have spent over 18 years actively working as a Shamanic Healer, Hypnotherapist, Reiki Master, Breathwork Facilitator, Teacher, Retreat Leader and Plant Medicine Practitioner. I spontaneously started doing shamanic journeying at the age of 19. I have helped thousands of my clients live beautiful lives, or at the very least, helped them understand at a deep level how this is possible.

If you wish to learn more about how to be a practitioner of the healing techniques outlined in this book, we can help. At our spiritual healing retreat center in Vilcabamba, Ecuador, my wife Dianna and I offer the following retreats: Reiki I to Reiki Master, Shamanistic Reiki Trainings and Plant Medicines with Breathwork Retreats. We also offer Individual and Couples' healings. We work closely with local indigenous healers.

If you wish to learn about entering the subtle realms of the subconscious, for your own benefit or the benefit of your clients—or would like to blow open your mind—we would love to hear from you and hopefully see you in the near future.

We also offer Shamanic Healing Sessions which include *Shamanic Energy Extractions*, via Zoom. Please visit our websites:

www.AlchemicalAyahuasca.com

www.SacredValleyRetreats.com

www.SpiritWisdomHealing.com

To help spread the Love, please leave an honest book review on Amazon. Thank you!

RECOMMENDED READING

Reading is the only shortcut that exists in this world.
It allows you to learn from the experience of others
Without the same difficulty they experienced.
~ RYAN HOLIDAY

*Atomic Habits: An Easy & Proven Way to Build Good Habits &
Break Bad Ones*—James Clear

Autobiography of a Yogi—Paramahansa Yogananda

Being Peace—Thich Nhat Hanh

*Cave and the Cosmos. Shamanic Encounters with Another
Reality*—Michael Harner

*Creative Visualization: Use the Power of Your Imagination to
Create What You Want in Your Life*—Shakti Gawain

*DMT-The Spirit Molecule: A Doctor's Revolutionary Research
into the Biology of Near-Death and Mystical Experiences*—Rick
Strassman

*Essential Healing: Hypnotherapy and Regression Based Practices to
Release the Emotional Pain and Drama Keeping You Stuck*—Paul
Aurand

Lessons in Courage: Peruvian Shamanic Wisdom for Everyday Life—Oscar Miro Quesada

Listening to Ayahuasca: New Hope for Depression, Addiction, PTSD and Anxiety—Rachel Harris

Hallucinogens and Shamanism—Michael Harner

Instant Healing: Mastering the Way of the Hawaiian Shaman Using Words, Images, Touch, and Energy—Serge Kahili King

Journey of Souls: Case Studies of Life Between Lives—Michael Newton

Just Breathe: Mastering Breathwork for Success in Life, Love, Business, and Beyond—Dan Brulé

Many Lives, Many Masters: The True Story of a Prominent Psychiatrist, His Young Patient, and the Past-Life Therapy That Changed Both Their Lives—Brian Weiss, MD

Mastering Your Hidden Self: A Guide to the Huna Way—Serge Kahili King

Peace in Every Step: The Path of Mindfulness in Every Step—Thich Nhat Hanh

Power vs. Force, The Hidden Determinants of Human Behavior—Dr. David R. Hawkins

Psycho-Cybernetics, A New Way to Get More Living Out of Life—Dr. Maxwell Maltz

Shamanic Journeying: A Beginner's Guide—Sandra Ingerman

Singing to the Plants: A Guide to Mestizo Shamanism in the Upper Amazon—Steven Bayer

Soul Retrieval: Mending the Fragmented Self—Sandra Ingerman

Supernatural: Meeting with the Ancient Teachers of Mankind—Graham Hancock

The Alchemist—Paul Coelho

The Ayahuasca Test Pilots Handbook: The Essential Guide to Ayahuasca Journeying—Chris Kilham

The Power of Now: A Guide to Spiritual Enlightenment—Eckhart Tolle

The Untethered Soul: The Journey Beyond Yourself—Michael Singer

The Way of the Shaman—Michael Harner

The Way of the Superior Man: A Spiritual Guide to Mastering the Challenges of Women, Work, and Sexual Desire—David Deida

Urban Shaman—Serge Kahili King

Zen Mind, Beginners Mind—Shunryu Suzuki

TESTIMONIALS

"Alan, Alan, Alan . . . I literally have NO WORDS! I enjoyed every second with him. My husband and I have worked with multiple "healers" and we consider him one of the best we have come across. There is no doubt in my mind that I will be working with him again. No doubt! He is also available for zoom/Skype during these uncertain times in case a person is unable to travel. It's something to consider as you view the website. If I could hang around Mount Shasta for months just to work with him . . . I would.

On to the good stuff . . . two days after our session with Alan, I noticed little triggers of mine had "magically" disappeared. There were a few things that popped up in my life that I know would have disturbed me to the core and I might have REACTED vs RESPONDED. I end up handling those triggers with more loving energy vs resistance. I knew it was the work. This is when I was extremely convinced that I would work with him again. He is a TRUE SHAMAN! His practices and techniques are real."

~ANGELA

"I first had the honor of meeting him in April of 2015 at a shamanic full moon retreat in the mountains near Santa Cruz, CA. He displayed such charisma and power, yet such gentleness and wisdom as a shamanic practitioner, I felt that I could trust him almost immediately. His ceremony was intentional, positive, joyful, healing, magical, full of beauty

219

and music. He played instruments from all over the world and sang gorgeous songs, encouraging others to find their voices and sing as well. It was one of my favorite weekends of my entire life.

Since then, I have put my trust in him as a shaman, teacher and healer, and have been moving through a lot of my own stuck trauma in preparation to become a healer myself. He led a trip to Peru in October of 2015, which was spectacular! We studied with Shipibo shamans in the Ucayali basin, and learned about the plant life of the jungle. This year, Alan taught me advanced and shamanistic Reiki, and attuned me to its healing vibrations at a sacred spring on Mt. Shasta. He has led me on many shamanic journeys and helped me to rid myself of blockages and limiting beliefs, so that I could tune into higher frequencies and be a more powerful healer."

~LAUREN

"I met Alan in 2012 when I had reached the end of my rope with western healing practices toward stress and emotional trauma.

I cannot say enough about the intensity of my experience following the first in-person appointment. Everyone's experience will be different . . . but, prior to, it had felt as though each step I took was equivalent to pushing a massive pallet of bricks uphill . . . and coming out of the experience felt essentially like a powerful pack of wolves and flock of birds had been unleashed from my heart all at once drawn out by a golden light . . . well, you get the idea. Rarely can one say that they have had that experience without the aid of psychedelics, and Alan helped guide me there with measured breathing and a calmed mind."

~JOHN JAMES

"It's hard to put into words what a session with Alan is like, as it's truly a unique experience. Let me just say I went for one thing, and he unearthed something completely different that I didn't realize was holding me back. He helped me connect the dots from an image I was seeing in a session to 2 miscarriages I had many years ago. I had no idea I was still holding onto that, and as soon as he said it, it was like a lightning bolt through my body—I knew it was the truth. It was a very emotional session, but I felt about a thousand pounds lighter afterwards. So, to me, the session was like magic . . . he works with guides to see what cannot be seen . . . what needs healing.

As soon as you are in his presence, you know there is something very special about him. He has such a profound gentleness and quiet strength, which rarely go together. His presence is of a very rare quality—he is just a really, really gifted healer."

~KAREN

"It was the remembrance of Alan's unconditional love and divine light that literally shined through his face, particularly his eyes, that brought a great shift within me—I was able to realize the love within that brought about a unifying energy that is bringing me closer to the realization of my divinity, another part of the healing work that occurred with Alan. It was an honor to work with him, and I am so appreciative of his healing support during this transformative journey."

~CHRISTA

"Alan is the most extraordinary healer I have ever worked with, which is not to diminish the excellence of the other talented healers I have worked with in the past. My life has improved radically since my first meeting with Alan. I have suffered from chronic anxiety and depression for much of my life, which Alan has all but cured through a combination of healing modalities. I have participated in several healing workshops and retreats offered by Alan including, Reiki treatments, Reiki Level 3 and Master Class, Shamanistic Reiki, as well as his weekend Meditation Retreats.

I think Alan is the closest thing to a Buddha/healer that I have ever met. His spiritual guidance and connection to spirit is unparalleled in my experience. From the moment he lays his hands on you, you know that a powerful current of compassionate healing is flowing your way and you will begin to see miraculous transformations in your life almost instantaneously. In addition to the energy work that he performs, Alan is an extraordinarily wise and loving spiritual guide. He has a soft low-key manner in the way he presents information, but the depth of his teachings and the positive effects they will have on your life are truly profound."

~RICARDO

"I had the good fortune of meeting with Alan for a Shamanic healing session and feel incredibly blessed and grateful to have connected with this gifted healer. His humility, authenticity, compassion, gentle directness, wisdom, grounding, reverence, guidance and humor all helped create a contained, safe, loving space where I could contact hidden, wounded parts of myself, tend to those early wounds and experience the joy of finding self-acceptance, self-love and embodied healing.

Alan's love for his work, his experience with different modalities and spiritual traditions were evident in the way he guided me through the session—I felt not just the wisdom and love of this individual being, but the wisdom and love of all his teachers and the generations carrying this healing medicine. Alan was able to connect with my heart, and in that connection, he helped me find the courage to get passed my limiting negative thought patterns, to overcome my resistance and ultimately to connect with and surrender to my own heart. I am eternally thankful to Alan for his loving facilitation and guidance—how can you thank someone enough for helping you restore your Self?"

~DESIRAE

"This session left me feeling whole and light. I would recommend this session to anyone who is looking to get rid of limiting beliefs/patters or needs healing of any kind. This healing will work well for beginners or people who have done substantial spiritual work.

Regardless of where you are on your journey, Alan meets you where you are and gives you the healing you need. Having worked with many spiritual healers I can say that Alan is such a natural and his healing is so gentle and effective.
This session was so powerful I felt like I was sitting right in front of Alan even though it was done via Zoom (energy is energy, distance doesn't really matter!)"

~ASH

"I attended the Reiki 1 & 2 retreat with Alan and Dianna, and it is hard to find words to express the profoundly healing and energetically shifting weekend I experienced. They are a remarkable couple with a beautiful love story, and their synergy created such a safe, nurturing, and powerful weekend full of ceremony, teaching, practicing, and community with a group of amazing humans! I also did an individual healing with Alan and experienced an incredible healing—a lot of deep work in a short amount of time. He is highly skilled, intuitive, and a true healer. I have found a new community here, and feel so blessed. I highly recommend any of Alan and Dianna's services! They have incredible integrity, authenticity, and wisdom."

~CHELLI

"I opted for a Zoom session with one of the co-founders, Alan. His grounded presence and deep human wisdom was immediately known & felt-I knew I was in the presence of a Master holding sacred space for healing. Alan is truly a gifted shaman & healer as well as a joy to engage with. His personal knowledge, deep wisdom, unique skills & mindful intention allowed for an amazing insight and shifts for me. I would highly recommend his Zoom services and look very forward to the Reiki & Breathwork retreats."

~BAMBI

"So many beautiful moments led by Alan and Dianna, that reached into the depths of my soul, hugging and healing every dark part of me that needed light. These two individuals are the light. Genuine. Beautiful. Non-Judging and Authentic! This encounter has made me embrace my calling with open arms and I'm choosing to walk in my truth and higher purpose of this beautiful thing called life. You have no idea what an invaluable gift that was to me. I am forever changed, forever grateful and forever blessed for experiencing these two beautiful souls and the new friendships that came out of the weekend. From the bottom of my heart, Thank you Alan and Dianna for welcoming me and for such an amazing time—I am looking forward to our next visit, really soon."

~ THERESA

NOTES

Made in the USA
Las Vegas, NV
17 February 2025

18260855R00138